# LIFE BY PERSONAL DESIGN

## Limitless Horizons

**SECOND EDITION**

Maria Napoli
Sue Roe

Kendall Hunt
publishing company

www.kendallhunt.com
*Send all inquiries to:*
4050 Westmark Drive
Dubuque, IA 52004-1840



ISBN 978-0-7575-9286-7



Printed in the United States of America
10 9 8 7 6 5 4 3

# Contents

*About the Author* v
*Prologue* vii

CHAPTER 1 The Magic of Mindfulness 1
CHAPTER 2 Protecting Your Life Space: Environmental Awareness 15
CHAPTER 3 Healthful Eating 31
CHAPTER 4 My Body, My Strength 43
CHAPTER 5 Rest, Relaxation, and Recreation: Restoring Balance 55
CHAPTER 6 Building Rewarding Relationships 65
CHAPTER 7 My Passion Discovery 79
CHAPTER 8 Personal Visioning 89
Your Future . . . Can Be Your Current Reality 101

# About the Author

Dr. Sue Roe is a highly respected professional and community leader, teacher, creative designer, skillful facilitator, and change agent. Dr. Roe is the managing partner of Performance Dimensions Consulting, LLC, and founder of the Consortium to Advance Integrative Healing and Wellness. She has a doctorate in public administration with an emphasis in administration and policy, additional graduate work in educational administration and instructional development, and a master's and bachelor's degree in nursing. Dr. Roe is a faculty associate at Arizona State University in the College of Nursing & Health Innovation and the School of Social Work and also teaches professional development courses at other colleges and universities. She has authored a nursing textbook and two chapters for a medical textbook on complementary and alternative medicine. Past publications also include guidebooks and publications on writing skills, the research process, management, and accreditation. Dr. Roe is currently involved in several projects that focus on holistic nursing, faculty development, healthcare program development, and grant writing. She is a sought-after presenter both locally and nationally on such topics as leadership, personal enrichment and wellness, and mastery. Dr. Roe has received several awards for her professional leadership activities and currently serves on a hospital and a foundation board.

Maria Napoli is an associate professor at Arizona Sate University. She has incorporated the practice of mindfulness in research, teaching, trainings and presentations at conferences nationally and internationally. She has developed mindfulness programs for elementary school children, undergraduate and graduate students including a graduate certificate in integrative health with a focus on mindfulness practice. It is her vision to bring mindfulness into education at all levels with the intention of supporting students to perform at their personal best with empathy and focus on quality of life. She has published journal articles and two books, *A Family Casebook: Problem Based Learning and Mindful Self Reflection* and *Tools for Mindful Living: Stepping Stones for Practice,* book and CD.

# Prologue

The journey you are about to embark upon, *Life by Personal Design: Limitless Horizons,* offers you the opportunity to transform your life. Many of us would agree that our lives can stand some improvement, and for some even a complete makeover! The key to approaching *Life by Personal Design* is appreciating that there are no limits to the changes you can make. By spending time personally exploring and experiencing the many new horizons found in this book, you will benefit from the life-changing activities that will help you realize greater happiness and success.

You begin this journey with your toolbox that includes various personal strategies you have used most of your life. Some of these may no longer serve you and are not useful; others you will keep. Throughout your travels in *Life by Personal Design: Limitless Horizons,* you will explore the contents of your toolbox. In each chapter you will have a decision to make: shall I keep, add to, and/or remove my personal life strategies? By doing this you will create ways to improve your life. You will become aware of what you are willing to do to make changes and you will discover what obstacles may be in your way. *Life by Personal Design* is unique. It offers you an integrated perspective and gives YOU the control to create a life design that will work best for you.

You start your journey with *The Magic of Mindfulness.* When you are mindful, you pay attention to experiences without judgment. You become aware! By practicing mindfulness there is no confusion about what is occurring in your life. You are completely engaged in the moment—not looking back or ahead. When you are living in the present you clear the path of the mindless chatter of "old tapes" that can keep you stuck in old thinking and behavior patterns. Approaching your life mindfully opens up a panorama of choices you may have never seen before.

In *Protecting Your Life Space: Environmental Awareness,* you will increase your awareness of your home, work, and community. Living in a chemical- and pollutant-free environment is the goal. Simple changes such as drinking water from stainless-steel bottles instead of plastic and reducing the amount of time you microwave to airing out your bed daily to prevent mites from breeding are just a few ways to become environmentally aware. You have control in more ways than you know to make safer and healthier choices in your living environment.

In *Healthful Eating,* you will explore the intimate relationship you have with the food you eat. You will examine not only what you eat, but identify your eating patterns and how certain foods make you feel both physically and emotionally. You will look at what draws you to certain foods and how food can provide you with energy or make you feel lethargic or acidic. Eating well and healthfully is one of the greatest gifts you can give yourself.

In *My Body, My Strength,* you will have a chance to go beyond the idea of thinking about your body as simply being made up of muscles and bones. Bodies are "mean energy machines" with the ability to endure years of abuse from lack of exercise, poor eating habits, and stress. Although all of us need some form of physical activity, different bodies have different needs and function at different energy levels. Finding the exercise, energy work, and activities that meet your body's needs is surely the way to strengthen it.

In *Rest, Relaxation, and Recreation: Restoring Balance,* you will be reminded of the need to nurture yourself. Finding ways to feel rested, creating opportunities for relaxation, and adding fun and frolic into your life is essential for maintaining balance. Many of us have forgotten how to play, have not created time for rest, suffer from insomnia, and cannot sit still long enough to relax. One day you may find yourself asking the question: where has all of my time gone? Remember, you cannot take time back, but you can make rest, relaxation, and recreation an integral part of your life.

In *Building Rewarding Relationships,* you will find a mirror to self-reflect on how you are impacted by the significant others in your life. Understanding how you developed your relationships with people can be an uphill hike when you factor in changes that occur in those relationships over time. Exploring how to improve your relationships and identifying those that may hold you back from transforming your life are the key ingredients to greater fulfillment.

In *My Passion Discovery,* you will examine what "makes you tick." You will ask yourself, am I in a rut, are things too routine, or am I lacking "color" in my life? You may wonder, am I moving through my life without direction, or not really focusing on what I really want to do? The hope is that when your journey reaches this far in the book, you will be ready to fully and mindfully answer these questions because you will be ready to create the "exciting new you"!

In *Personal Visioning,* you will be prepared to set intention in your life. You will be willing to determine what you want to have happen. You will have insight into how to remove the obstacles that get in your way. You will know what you have to do to engage in and live your personal vision. And, you will be excited and energized about your limitless horizons!

We are delighted to share *Life by Personal Design: Limitless Horizons* with you. We encourage you to take advantage of the many opportunities found in this book to pursue your limitless horizons. You can begin with the Personal Design Quality of Life Wheel found on the next page. Look at the sections of the Wheel and think about how well you are doing in each. For example, are you happy with your current career or how well you are doing in school? Are you satisfied with the state of your health and well-being? Have you identified what makes you feel passionate?

In each section put a percentage of how well you are doing. For example, in the health section you may feel your diet is pretty good but you find you are not exercising enough, so you give yourself a 60%. Or, in the environment section, you are happy with where you live but know you could be more conscious of the "greening" of the environment, so you give yourself a 70%. Or, you are now in school and find you have little time for rest and recreation so you give yourself a 45% in this section.

Once you have filled in the Wheel you are ready to start reading the book. You have provided yourself an assessment of your current state. Think about this as you venture forth into each of the chapters, completing the reading and activities.

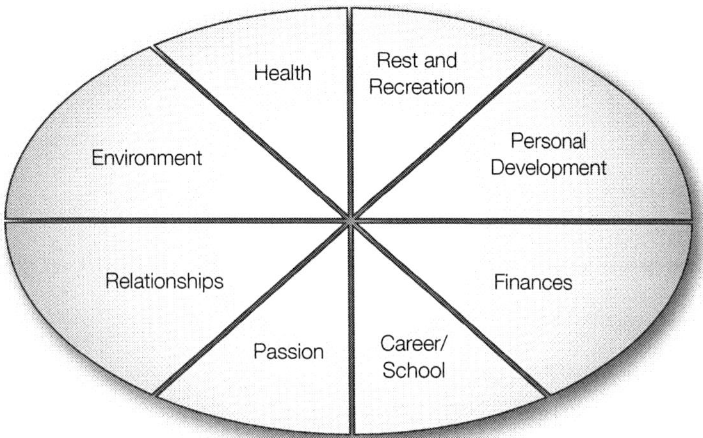


Personal Design Quality of Life Wheel

We are confident that this journey through the interactive experiences in each of the chapters will help you create ways to improve and enhance the quality of your life.

Our wish is for you to have days filled with fun, meaning, and health, but, most of all, our desire is for you to live that special life you designed for yourself!

*Maria and Sue*

# CHAPTER 1

# The Magic of Mindfulness

## Limitless Horizons

*You are here now; see, hear, feel, touch, and taste every experience!*

Mindfulness can be described as the acceptance of your moment-to-moment experience without internal or external filters. You are often stimulated by your internal mindless chatter, pushing you back into the past or propelling you toward the future, with both taking you out of the present moment.

From the minute you are born, your perceptions of the world around you are shaped by the interactions of significant people in your life. Research has found that children who are raised with caregivers who are attentive and accepting develop enhanced reflective and regulative skills. This ability to pay attention is the road to developing mindfully (1, p. 180).

How did you get to the point of passing through life without noticing the obvious, letting precious opportunities drift away without awareness? Let's take a look at how you begin your life mindfully then take an about-face into mindlessness. It's interesting to note that when you enter the world you approach everyday situations mindfully. As an infant, mindfulness was inherent in your everyday communication with the internal and outside worlds. You listened to your body's cues—hunger, pain, need for touch—and instincts. Infants are integrally connected to their experiences; whether they are comfortable or uncomfortable experiences, they all matter. As you increase your interaction with others you gradually seem to decrease being present, frequently getting caught in the past or having expectations about the future. There are probably many reasons for this, such as being stuck in the fight-or-flight mind-set due to stress, adhering to the norms of family and society, and trying to meet the expectations of others. Let's explore the process of your life cycle—moving from mindfulness to mindlessness and coming back to living mindfully together—in this chapter.

When you are mindful you pay attention to your environment—smells, tastes, sights, sounds, smiles and frowns, happy and sad emotions—and feel the energy of those around you.

Before language is learned, infants begin to mirror and internalize the nonverbal emotions and experiences of their caregivers. Mindfulness moves us into discomfort rather than away from it (2) and in so doing we can move on and experience those moments rather than being stuck in avoidance. It is no surprise that adults often ponder the wish to be a child again—"oh to be free as a child again, without a care in the world." In actuality, as a child it was your full engagement with experiences, both comfortable and uncomfortable, that gave you that sense of freedom. The reality is that you can reconnect with those basic experiences when you are mindful. Where do you get stuck? Unfortunately, in the modern world, infants

move quickly from being mindful into mindlessness as they enter childhood.

As infants move *toward early childhood*, the privilege of embracing the world on their own terms begins to change. Children soon begin to feel the rejection and judgment of family and social norms, which can take them out of their experience and into others' expectations of what is acceptable. Thus, children begin to repress feelings to gain the approval of others. Recently, researchers are studying mindful children, with positive results. Children who practiced mindfulness were found to have decreased anxiety and increased selective attention (3). Elementary-age children who were taught mindfulness skills were found to have a greater capacity for attention and awareness in the school day as compared to children in the control group (4). In addition, mindful children in a school-based mindful awareness practice program who were less well regulated showed gains in behavioral regulation, metacognition, and overall global executive control (5, p. 71). Researchers are also finding that children with chronic illness can benefit from mindfulness to deal with physical illness, thus reducing their use of medication (6).

Of course children need guidance, yet too often they are swept away into the adult world of mindlessness where restriction, judgments, expectations, and autocratic discipline occur more frequently than choice, acceptance, and interactive discussion. Mothers who exhibited high control and little dialogue with their children correlated positively with the mothers' rating of their children's problems, whereas those with lessened control and more dialogue correlated negatively with the mothers' child-problem ratings. These results show a viable connection between the mothers' mindfulness and their perception of their child's problems (7, p. 233). Children 9 to 12 years old who participated in 12-week mindfulness-based cognitive therapy for children reported a significant reduction in attention problems, and parents reported their children having fewer conduct or anger management problems (8).

As children move along the developmental timeline, they learn to conform—to exhibit emotions and behaviors to meet the approval of adults—and by the time they reach adolescence those children are stuck in mindlessness. The spontaneous developmental behavioral and emotional spurts during adolescence are often frowned upon, placing adolescents in a "box" where they often rebel to be free. Adolescents experience a surge of emotions which can be a positive experience as they explore relationships with friends and love relationships. It can be helpful to teach adolescents mindfulness skills to increase their emotional regulation skills. Results of the mindfulness BREATHE program found that adolescents reported reductions in negative attitudes and increases in feelings of calmness, relaxation, and self-acceptance compared to controls (9). Adolescents who participated in a mindfulness-based stress reduction program reported reduced symptoms of anxiety, depression, and physical distress as well as increased self-esteem and sleep quality (10). Results of a mindfulness-enhanced family-strengthening program found that mothers showed

sizable improvement in their anger management skills, and were more in tune with their adolescent children's emotions (11, p. 214).

Simply stated, when adolescents are present and accepts his or her experience without judgment, they begin to form healthy relationships with themselves and significant others in their lives.

As *an adult,* your experience with the outside world and the many roles you have increase your dependence on language and social norms, which can impede acknowledging and accepting your experiences without judgment. It is important for you as an adult to understand the nuances of your experiences by paying attention to your senses, body language, and instincts, which came easily to you as a child. A study using body movement and gestures as cues to emotions in younger and older adults found that younger adults had fewer errors in identifying emotions expressed than the older adults (12). One might thus infer that as you get older, you pay less attention to your experiences.

Mindfulness increases your ability to be nonjudgmental, thereby increasing your ability to experience emotions in a more positive way. A study assessing emotional regulation in response to distressing, positive, and mixed-emotion film clips found that participants in the mindfulness intervention group reported significantly greater positive affect in response to the positive film clips and more adaptive regulation in response to the mixed-emotion clips (13, p. 72). Being attentive to and accepting of your everyday experiences is a basic tenet of mindfulness.

"Mindfulness is essentially about waking up to what the present moment offers" (14, p. 272). Even the uncomfortable moments are valuable to you, helping you grow into an evolved human being. Repressing and avoiding those experiences will limit you and take up unnecessary space in your life. You give the thoughts and emotions that are attached to those experiences permission to haunt you over and over again. In some respects, you have thrown the baby out with the bath water with the advancement of technology—automation, television, the Internet, and iPods—keeping you in high gear. Don't misunderstand the point: These conveniences are amazing tools that can open doors for you to be present. Yet a problem arises when you crowd your mind, use up your time, and move too fast to simply notice what's happening in your moment-to-moment experience.

Can you imagine showing up in your very important life noticing and accepting all of your experiences, whatever they may be? Think of a child at play. The child is most likely completely absorbed in the moment, laughing and romping. Suddenly the child takes a fall, cries, and seeks out a hug. The child immediately returns to being immersed in play again, not looking back or ahead but fully engaged in the experience. Children are better able to experience their discomfort and then let it go. Embracing the experience of enjoying a beautiful sunset as much as the feelings of rejection is the essence of practicing mindfulness. Life does throw you curves without notice, yet it is those curves that are the stepping-stones to transformation—the bigger the challenge, the bigger the transformation. The same is true for capturing the pleasant experiences that surround you. These experiences fill the soul with possibility, joy, and magic. How do you get to this place of living mindfully?

When you are mindful, you open up the opportunity to be a nonjudgmental witness to your present experience. The result is "CHOICE." When you pay attention to your experience you have a CHOICE to *do something or do nothing*. Trying out new experiences with the eyes of a child contributes to the magic of personal transformation in life. You have the privilege of accepting each experience that life grants you, whether or not your present experience elicits positive or negative thoughts and emotions. You have the choice to react or respond to your experiences. When you react you ignite the stress response are prone to judgment, expectations, and avoidance of the experience. Your body reacts

© Luba V Nel, 2011. Used under license from Shutterstock, Inc.

to the alarm by pouring stress hormones into the system, slowing down digestion, increasing the heart rate, and contracting muscles. On the other hand, when you *respond* to your experiences, rather than react, you embrace them without judgment or expectation. Although you may endure discomfort, the benefit of freedom and letting go are what you gain. One thing you can be assured of at all times: the experience is yours and only you have the power to choose what to do with that experience.

When you accept yourself without judgment you are better able to accept others without judgment. Research has found that when couples are mindful, they are able to deal with conflictual discussions with lower anxiety and less anger and hostility. Individuals with greater mindfulness skills had higher levels of satisfaction with their emotional relationships (15, p. 495–496). The greatest gift we can have when we live mindfully is the capacity for compassion and empathy. When you accept your own joy and suffering you are better able to accept it in others. Opening the doors to give and receive love is enhanced when you are mindful, as you create more space for acceptance and close the door on judgment.

© Haywiremedia, 2011. Used under license from Shutterstock, Inc.

Through your acceptance of your experiences you carve out the path for happiness. How you show up for your experience will determine the outcome. The more time you spend accepting your moment-to-moment experience without judgment, the greater the opportunity for genuine happiness. When we are not stuck in the past or ruminating about the future, we have more time to enjoy what is happening now.

The following four-step MAC Mindfulness Model will help you focus on each experience by *(1) empathically acknowledging each experience; (2) intentionally paying attention to your senses, thoughts, emotions, and instincts regarding each experience; (3) accepting your experience without judgment or internal or external filters; and (4) taking action toward change as you make a decision about your experience* (16). As you move through the four MAC steps, remember to stay focused on your breath. Let's enjoy the following experience.

Close your eyes and bring your attention to your breath. Notice the rise of your belly on the inhale and fall on the exhale.

- *Empathically acknowledge all aspects of the breathing experience by noticing the nuances of your breathing.*
- *Intentionally pay attention to your senses, thoughts, emotions, and instincts regarding your breathing experience.* You may notice shallow, rapid, short, or deep breathing.

- *Accept your breathing experience without judgment.* Now gently open your eyes and look around you. What do you notice? Take in this awareness.
- *Take action* as to how you would like to proceed with your breathing experience.

This is a simple exercise you can do daily to help you stay in the moment and begin bringing mindfulness into your life. The breath is your life source, taking on its direction by how you live your life. You may notice that your breath is short when anxious, rapid when fearful, and that you sometimes stop your breath when you are in shock or feeling aghast. This gift of life, your breath, is your ticket to living a mindful life. Paying attention to your breath does not take up extra time or cost any money, does not involve the cooperation of anyone other than yourself, and offers a multitude of bonuses that add quality to your life. This is the best deal you will ever have. Take it!

As you reflect on developing your mindfulness practice, it becomes evident that we begin our lives mindfully and are fully engaged in our experiences, using our senses, emotions, and instincts. The increase in reacting to situations and the expectations of self and others, the focus on language versus our senses, and judgment of self as well as by others moves us into mindlessness. But all is not lost; as an adult you can experience the world once again with eyes of a child, with freshness and excitement, responding to the nuances of your experiences with nonjudgmental acceptance. Why not embrace all of your experiences? They are the most valuable gift you can give yourself to increase the quality of your life and experience the limitless horizons that await you!

## *Life Design Mindfulness Checklist*

When I am having a conversation, I speak before the person is finished talking. Describe to what extent this statement applies to you.

______________________________________________
______________________________________________
______________________________________________

Prepare and eat a meal, noticing each detail while you are eating, Describe your experience.

______________________________________________
______________________________________________
______________________________________________

I notice I live in the past or ruminate about things that have happened. Describe to what extent this statement applies to you.

______________________________________________
______________________________________________
______________________________________________

When I pay attention to my body, I notice . . .

______________________________________________
______________________________________________
______________________________________________

When I pay attention to my breath, I notice . . .

______________________________________________
______________________________________________
______________________________________________

### My Three Strategies

What I am willing to do today to be successful in creating change in my life so I can live mindfully:

1. ______________________________________________
______________________________________________
2. ______________________________________________
______________________________________________
3. ______________________________________________
______________________________________________
______________________________________________

## Designer Activities

*(These* ***activities*** *will help you achieve your* ***strategies****.)*

*Silence*

1. Carve out an hour a day for one week where you can practice total silence (turn off phone, music, television).
2. Following your experience, describe the awareness in a journal.
3. Close your eyes after reflecting on what you have written in your journal, breathe, and integrate the experience.

*Mindful Eating*

1. For one week eat one meal per day in silence.
2. Notice the food when you are preparing it (e.g., color, smells, textures).
3. Sit in a comfortable chair and clear your eating space of magazines, mail, and so forth.
4. Notice the food with your eyes as you bring the food toward your mouth.
5. Savor the smells of the food.
6. Chew your food 25 to 50 times before swallowing.
7. Listen to the sounds of your chewing and notice the sensations in your mouth.

*Mindful Walking*

1. For one week take a walk for 15 minutes each day.
2. Scan the feelings in your body front and back from head to toe while walking.
3. Notice what your body is communicating.

*My Thought Awareness Reflective Journal*

1. For one week pay attention to your thoughts.
2. Keep a journal of positive and negative thinking and observe with mindfulness.

| Positive Thoughts | Negative Thoughts |
|---|---|
| | |

*Stimulating Senses*

1. Step outdoors into nature.
2. *Smell* and breathe the air softly and deeply.
3. Close your eyes and *listen* to the sounds of nature.
4. *Feel* the temperature of the air on your body.
5. Focus your gaze on an element in nature; experience it without distraction.
6. Choose one element in nature to *touch*, and feel the texture.
7. Describe your experience.

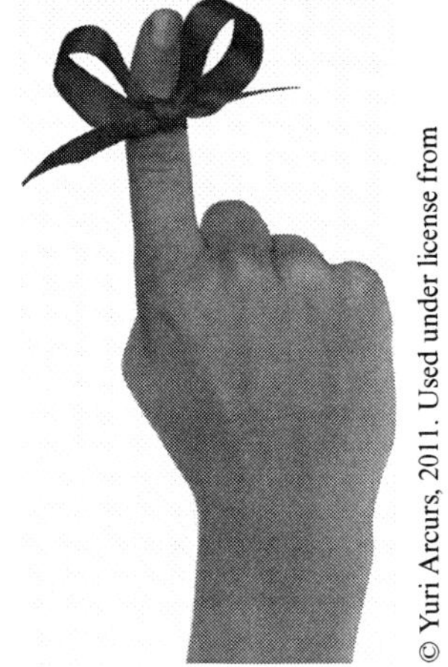



Remember, you can begin living mindfully by using the following MAC guidelines.

1. Focus on your breath.
2. Acknowledge your experience.
3. Pay attention to your thoughts and feelings, body, and instincts.
4. Accept your awareness without judgment.
5. Take action and integrate the experience and your awareness of feelings, sensations, and thoughts toward change.

# Magic of Mindfulness
## REFLECTIVE JOURNAL

## Reference


(1) Ryan, R. M., Brown, K. W., & Creswell, J. D. (2003). How Integrative is attachment theory? Unpacking the meaning and significance of felt security. *Psychological Inquiry 14*(1), 177–182.

(2) Claxton, G. (2005). Mindfulness, learning and the brain. *Journal of Rational-Emotive & Cognitive Behavior Therapy, 23,* 301–314

(3) Napoli, M., Krech, P. & Holley, L. C. (2005). Mindfulness training for elementary school students: The attention academy. *Journal of Applied School Psychology, 21*(1), 2005

(4) http://www.auroraschool.org/mindfulness.html

(5) Flook, L., Smalley, S. L., Kitil, M. J., Galla, B. M., Kaiser-Greenland, S., Locke, L., Ishijima, E., & Kasari, C. (2010). Effects of mindful awareness practice on executive functions in elementary school children. *Journal of Applied School Psychology 26,* 70–95.

(6) Ott, M. J. (2002, September/October). Mindfulness meditation in pediatric clinical practice, *28*(5), 487–490.

(7) Williams, K. L., & Wahler, R. G. (2010). Are mindful parents more authoritative and less authoritarian? An analysis of clinic-referred mothers. *Journal of Child and Family Studies, 19,* 230–235.

(8) Semple, R. J., Lee, J., Rosa, D., & Miller, L. F. (2010). A Randomized Trial of Mindfulness-Based Cognitive Therapy for Children: Promoting of Mindful Attention to Enhance Social-Emotional Resiliency in Children. *Journal Children and Family Studies, 19*, 218–229.

(9) Broderick,learning2breathe.org/background/parent

(10) Biegel, G., Brown, K. W., Shapiro, S. L., & Schubert, C. M. (2009). Mindfulness-based stress reduction for the treatment of adolescent psychiatric outpatients: A randomized clinical trial. *Journal of Consulting and Clinical Psychology*, *77*(5), 855–866.

(11) Coatsworth, D. J., Duncan, L. G., Greenberg, M. T., & Nix, R. L. (2010). Changing parent's mindfulness, child management skills and relationship quality with their youth: Results from a randomized pilot intervention trial. *Journal of Child and Family Studies, 19,* 203–217.

(12) Montepare, Zaitchik, & Albert. (1999, Summer). The use of body movement and gestures as cues to emotions in younger and older adults. *Journal of Nonverbal Behavior, 23*(2), 133–152.

(13) Erisman, S. M., & Roemer, L. (2010). A preliminary investigation of the effects of experimentally-induced mindfulness on emotional responding to film clips. *Emotion, 10*, 72–82.

(14) Brown, K. W., Ryan, R. M., & Creswell, J. D. (2007). Addressing fundamental questions about mindfulness. *Psychological Inquiry, 18*(4), 272–281.

(15) Barnes, S., Brown, K. W., Krusemark, E. K., Campbell, & Rogge, R. D. (2007). The role of mindfulness in romantic relationship satisfaction and responses to relationship stress. *Journal of Marital and Family Therapy, 33*(4), 482–500.

(16) Napoli, M. (2007). *Tools for mindful living: Steppingstones for practice*. Dubuque, IA: Kendall/Hunt Publishing.

## Other Readings to Explore

Arch, J. J., & Craske, M. G. (2006). Mechanisms of mindfulness: Emotional regulation following a focused breathing induction. *Behavior Research and Therapy*, *44*, 1849–1958.

Berceli, D., & Napoli, M. (2006). Mindfulness-based trauma-prevention program for social work professionals. *Journal of Complementary Health Practice Review, 11,* 153–165.

Carson, S. H., & Langer, E. J. (2006). Mindfulness and self-acceptance. *Journal of Rational-Emotive & Cognitive Behavior Therapy, 24*, 29–43.

Davidson, R., Kabat-Zinn, J., Schumacher, J., Rosenkranz, M., Muller, D., Santorelli, S. F., Urbanowski, F., Harrington, A., Bonus, K., & Sheridan, J. F. (2003, July/August). Alterations in brain and immune function produced by mindfulness meditation. *American Psychosomatic Society, 65*(4), 564–570.

Ditto, B., Eclache, M., & Goldman, N. (2006). Short-term autonomic and cardiovascular effects of mindfulness body scan meditation. *Annals of Behavioral Medicine, 32*, 227–234.

Lundh, L. (2005). The role of acceptance and mindfulness in the treatment of insomnia. *Journal of Cognitive Psychotherapy, 19*, 29–39.

Shapiro, S. L., Brown, K. W., & Biegel, G. M. (2007). Teaching self-care to caregivers: Effects of mindfulness-based stress reduction on the mental health of therapists in training. *Training and Education in Professional Psychology, 1*(2), 105–115.

Tacon, A. M., McComb, J., Caldera, Y., & Randolph, P. (2003). Mindfulness meditation, anxiety reduction and heart disease. *Family Community Health, 26*(1), 25–33.

CHAPTER 2

© Xtremer, 2011. Used under license from Shutterstock, Inc.

# Protecting Your Life Space: Environmental Awareness

*The sun, the moon and the stars would have disappeared long ago . . . had they happened to be within the reach of predatory human hands.*

*~Havelock Ellis, The Dance of Life, 1923*

As you move along in your day, you eat, wash, drink, and breathe. Most likely you take these simple activities for granted. All too often our overindulgence in today's world has made these basic essentials for healthy living a rare commodity. We are polluting our food, water, and air, contributing to our demise by increasing our susceptibility to preventable illnesses such as cancer, autoimmune deficiency, respiratory illness, and heart disease. Approximately 40% of deaths worldwide are caused by water, air, and soil pollution due to environmental degradation and growth in world population, which contribute to an increase in human disease (1). The field of environmental medicine is becoming widespread as more people suffer from illnesses due to airborne chemicals in the workplace, community, and home. All living things are interdependent upon each other. Plants need carbon dioxide that humans produce; humans need oxygen that plants produce; and animals, birds, fish, and insects provide a balance in the ecology of our air, water, and land. In terms of keeping yourself alive and well, you might look at what your body is made up of: 65% oxygen, 18% carbon, 10% hydrogen, 3% nitrogen, 1.5% calcium; 1% phosphorous, and 1.5% remaining minerals (2). All of these elements are available in nature, yet are dwindling due to our greed and reckless violence toward our planet. Ecologists say that it is not too late to reverse this trend, yet many people seem oblivious to the problems we are creating that can be prevented if we pay attention to our behavior and begin taking action in our own lives.

© violetkaipa, 2011. Used under license from Shutterstock, Inc.

### *Air*

The leading causes of air pollution are motor vehicle emissions, chemical plants, coal-fired power plants, oil refineries, petrochemical plants, nuclear waste disposal activities, incinerators, and large livestock farms (3). We can prevent the increase in premature deaths, asthma, and mercury contamination by demanding stricter power plant regulations. With so many chemicals being introduced, the incidence of multiple chemical sensitivity (MCS) is increasing. Children are at greater risk, as their tissues grow rapidly and their detoxification systems are immature (4). You cannot control the quality of air in your neighborhoods, yet you do have some control in your home. For example, plants provide oxygen, and installing wood or stone floors instead of carpets; changing air filters; and controlling dust in air ducts, fans, draperies, and shades and mites in beds can all contribute to cleaner air in your home. Your body is increasingly affected by multiple chemicals in daily living, yet you are often most likely unaware of their detrimental effects.

As an adult you may be aware of the changes in your daily functioning, yet frequently ignore them due to time constraints placing your attention on your routines and the activities that take precedence. For example, you may have a general feeling of unwellness and visit your physician, yet your physician cannot find anything wrong. Illness related to chemicals is rapidly becoming a problem, yet we are often at a loss as to how to identify and treat diseases related to chemicals. Recently, pollution-related illnesses are being studied in the field of environmental medicine. Researchers are beginning to identify what pollution does at the cellular level, the level of biochemistry where energy is produced. Some problems resulting from environmental pollution are:

| Problem | Symptoms |
|---|---|
| Brain fog | Poor concentration |
| Autoimmunity | Frequent infections (yeast and fungal) |
| Asthma | Respiratory distress |
| Emotional instability | Mood swings: anger, frustration |
| Recurrent muscle strains | Strain in tendons, ligaments |
| Sleep disorders | Waking between 1–3 AM |

(5)

When you are exposed to volatile organic compounds (VOCs), such as petro-chemicals and other forms of commercial-solvent-type chemicals, these chemicals are rapidly sponged out of the bloodstream and stored in the fatty tissues of your body. Your brain, like the liver and heart, has a rich blood supply and high fat content, and thus the brain is a primary target for chemicals to hide. By the time these environmental pollutants are recognized, it is too late for treatment (6). The illnesses in the following diagram could be prevented by eliminating exposure to chemical pollution.

#### Chronic Illnesses Significantly Associated with Chemicals

Now that we have looked at some of the problems, let's take a look at some solutions that can improve your physical, mental, and aesthetic environment. Your immune system is able to fight off viruses and bacteria, yet is not able to help eliminate or recognize toxic metals in your body. Using an infrared sauna

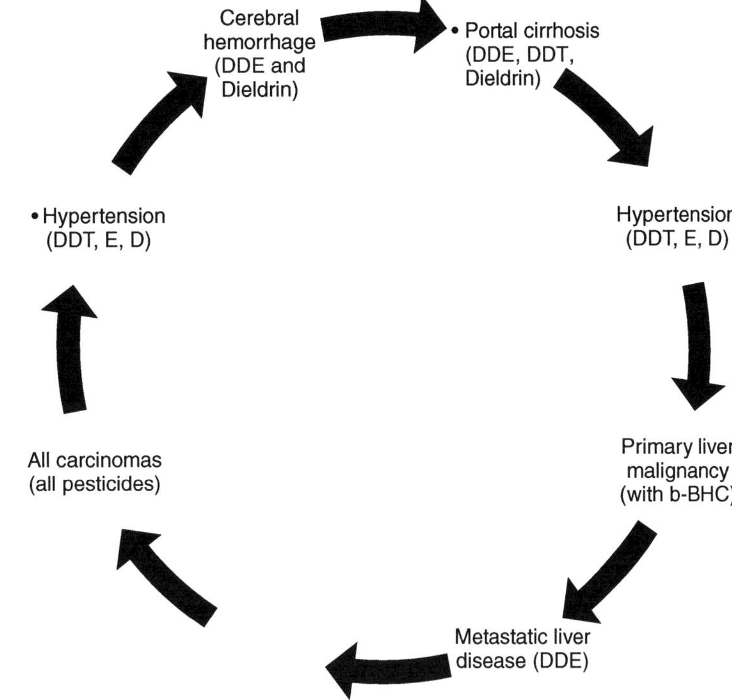


***There's so much pollution in the air now that if it weren't for our lungs there'd be no place to put it all (7).***

is a simple way to eliminate chemicals from your body. Because the infrared sauna's heat penetrates deeply (up to 1 3/4 inches compared to the traditional sauna, which only penetrates approximately 1/8 of an inch), your body can get a good detoxifying sweat going at about 120 degrees as compared to the 180 degrees required from a traditional sauna.

**Benefits of an Infrared Sauna**

- Causes weight loss (without having to lift a finger)
- Helps treat cellulite
- Improves your immune system
- Improves your strength and vitality
- Helps cure several skin diseases, such as eczema, psoriasis, and acne
- Strengthens the cardiovascular system
- Helps control your blood pressure
- Detoxifies your body
- Gives you more energy and relieves stress
- Helps treat burns and scars
- Relieves pain (joint pain, sore muscles, arthritis)
- Helps control your cholesterol level
- Helps treat bronchitis

*Source: (8)*

When your body is given the opportunity to do its job, it has the innate capacity to discharge toxins and store nutrients. Your lungs, liver, kidneys, and skin are the key to your waste elimination. If you give these organs a chance to do their job, you are on the road to being pollution-free.

**Keep Your Body Pollution-Free**

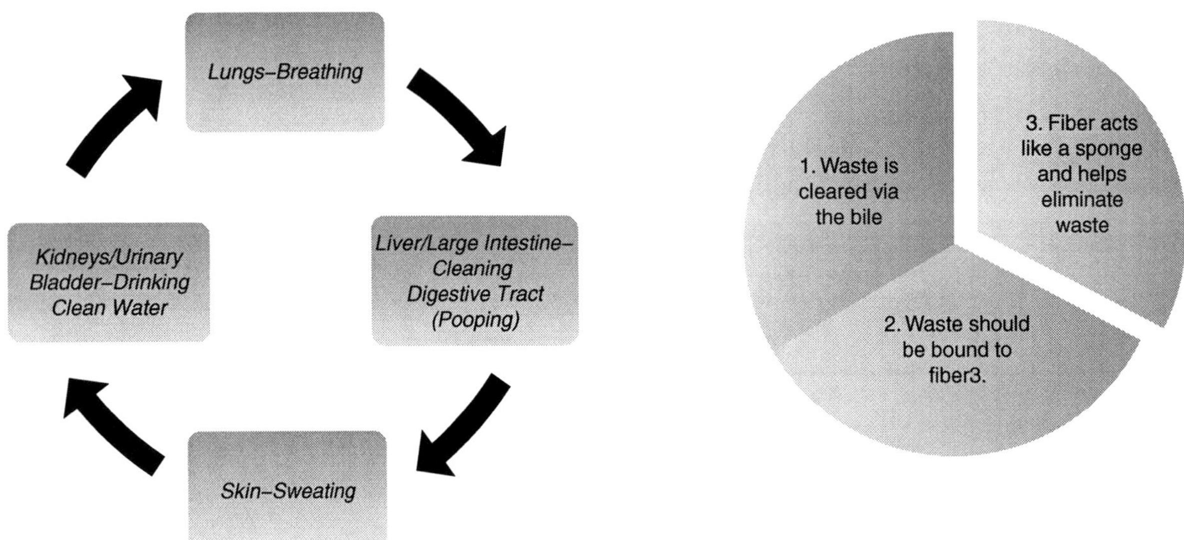


How does fiber work to help your body eliminate pollution? If your fiber intake is deficient, then waste will be reabsorbed back into your portal vein and lymphatic chain (think immune system). Additionally, if there is an overgrowth of bad bacteria, they can facilitate reabsorption of cellular waste, pollution, and excess hormones back into your body (9).

There is hope, and you can make a difference in your personal life, home, work, and community. When you are mindful of what you eat and how you use energy, and protect yourself by using chemical-free products, you begin to create the healthy life you deserve.

## *Your Home*

"Organic chemicals are widely used as ingredients in household products. Paints, varnishes, and wax all contain organic solvents, as do many cleaning, disinfecting, cosmetic, degreasing, and hobby products" (10). Walk around your house and notice your surroundings. You may initially take in the decorations, furniture, and artifacts that you have accumulated over the years.

© radoma, 2011. Used under license from Shutterstock, Inc.

Now take another walk around your house, this time taking a closer look in your cabinet drawers, closets, refrigerator, ceiling fans, and underneath your sink. You most likely will be surprised at what you find. You might say to yourself, "This place needs a good cleaning." Ok, if this is the case, go to your cleaning supply bath and cosmetic cabinets and examine the ingredients that are contained in the products you have been using. My guess is that most of the ingredients include chemicals that you cannot even pronounce. If you are cleaning your countertops and tables where you eat and prepare food, you are probably ingesting those chemicals. If you are cleaning your floors, you are taking them in through your skin if you walk barefoot. Interesting thoughts?

***There is a sufficiency in the world for man's need but not for man's greed.***

*~Mohandas K. Gandhi*

**Solutions to Protect Your Home**

- Make cleaning products from aromatherapy ingredients.
- Clean more often.
- Check labels.
- Ask more questions.
- Cleaning strategies such as avoiding the use of hot water, diluting each detergent as much as possible, and applying soft, non-acidic or non-abrasive detergents for a few minutes have been recommended to reduce exposure to detergents (11).
- Use cosmetics and creams without chemicals.
- Choose carpets with natural fibers.
- Choose clothing with natural fibers.
- Invest in an air purifier.
- Buy energy-efficient appliances.
- Switch to energy-efficient light bulbs.

Reducing your water temperature to 120°F slows mineral buildup and corrosion in your water heater and pipes. This helps your water heater last longer and operate at its maximum efficiency (12).

- Arrange furniture with feng shui and purchase ecologically friendly materials.
- Bring in more air from outdoors.
- Safely clean your home.

***Check out these simple recipes and take another step toward going green***

- All-Purpose Surface Cleaner Mix together equal parts white vinegar and salt. Scrub surfaces with a natural cleaning cloth.
- Cookware Cleaner Coarse salt does wonders for scouring copper pans and ceramic baking dishes.
- Disinfectant Mix 1/2 cup of borax powder with 1 gallon of hot water. Add a few drops of fragrant essential oil such as thyme, rosemary, or lavender. Store the mixture in a labeled spray bottle.
- Floor Scrubber To scrub out tough messes and stains, use washing soda and rinse well. For lighter washing, dilute 1 cup washing soda in 1 gallon of warm or hot water. Add a few tablespoons of vinegar or lemon juice for extra shine.

© Sergej Khakimullin, 2011. Used under license from Shutterstock, Inc.

### *Water*

The importance of providing your body with clean water cannot be overestimated. The time when your body could be nourished by drinking water from the tap or local rivers is long gone. Our rivers today are full of pollutants such as lead, aluminum, sodium fluoride, bacteria and viruses, chlorine, chloroform, MTBE (rocket fuel), pesticides, treated and filtered waste water, antibiotics, and antidepressants, to name a few. These pollutants cause fatigue, diminished cellular performance, and stunted cellular growth (13). Illnesses related to polluted drinking water are extensive, such as malaria, hepatitis, and other viruses. People die every day from drinking polluted water. The number of people lacking clean water is astounding. It is estimated that 1.2 billion people lack clean water, and water-borne infections account for 80% of all infectious diseases. A shocking Associated Press investigation found various pharmaceuticals in the drinking supplies of at least 41 million Americans. Even extremely diluted concentrations of pharmaceutical residues harm fish, frogs, and other aquatic species in the wild, and human cells fail to grow normally when exposed to trace concentrations of certain drugs (14).

The fact remains that we need to conserve the clean water we have and find ways to prevent polluting this essential commodity that we need to survive.

Take a moment and think about water more consciously.

- Drink bottled water.
- Conserve water when taking a shower, brushing your teeth, and so forth.
- Conserve water by using plants indigenous to your environment.
- Drink plenty of water daily to nourish and flush toxins from your body. Drink water from glass or stainless steel containers, instead of plastic, and install reverse osmosis filters if possible.

### *Land*

The foods you eat today often contain chemicals, either from the soil they were grown on or preservatives to sustain shelf life. One rule to follow when you are shopping for food is to avoid products that have chemicals as well as products with sugar and corn sweeteners. It is astounding how many products have these additives. Shopping the outer perimeters of the store where fresh foods are usually displayed instead of the middle isles where canned and boxed foods are shelved may help you make better choices. When you think about food only a century ago, you might visualize foods that were grown by the families who harvested them instead of a supermarket. It likely that those foods were not full of pesticides

© moomsabuy, 2011. Used under license from Shutterstock, Inc.

and that they supplied vitamins and minerals to help grow healthy cells in the body. The Environmental Protection Agency has approved 350 ingredients for food uses—200 of which account for 98% of the pesticides currently applied to agricultural products, many of them polluting water and killing plants and wildlife. "Farm workers who mix, load or apply certain pesticides have contracted serious illnesses and in some cases died from direct exposure, according to health officials (15)

In order for your body to be healthy, you need to have a greater percentage of alkalinity versus acidity. When our bodies are acidic, we are more susceptible to illness, as the balance is disrupted. Your body becomes acidic when it is exposed to non-foods such as chemicals, excess fats, and stress. Organic foods are a great way to support alkalinity in your bloodstream and within your cells. Organic foods have a higher nutrient density than conventional foods, higher antioxidant potential, higher enzyme capacity, and higher energy potential and are typically farmed in humane and sustainable ways without environmental pollution. When you maintain a happy and emotionally balanced life, you support your body's alkalinity.

Consuming large amounts of foods and eating foods with preservatives and chemicals contributes to the growing obesity epidemic in children and adults. Obesity is rapidly becoming one of the most deadly environmental illnesses. Unlike years ago, where famine killed thousands of people, today human beings live in the age of obesity—too much food and food that does not nourish the body and often contaminates it. In a survey of 360 articles published between January 1989 and April 2009, 12 major newspapers in the United States, Canada, and the United Kingdom reported that obesity is a lifestyle problem, yet individuals, governments, and industry need to share a role in addressing the modern environment (16). Your body has amazing innate intelligence. It knows exactly where to send the nutrients it receives through food, vitamins, and minerals ingested by eating and drinking.

### *Save Our Children*

Life has changed dramatically for children today. The days seem long lost when children found complete joy in the fresh air, playing outdoors without a thought of video games, iPods, or television. The more children play indoors, the more their connection to nature dwindles. The media does not help, with its advertising of technological products, and parents who are overworked often depend upon the technology of electronics to keep children busy. In addition, the increase in crimes against children may contribute to parents wanting their children to be safe indoors, sacrificing play in nature. "In a typical week, only 6 percent of children ages nine to thirteen play outside on their own; bike riding is down 31 since 1995; 90 percent of inner-city children do not know how to swim, and 34 percent have never been to a beach. Schools have canceled field trips, have buildings with no windows and many have eliminated outdoor or all physical education programs (17, p. 4).

The effects of outdoor pollution on children's health cannot be underestimated. Children 6 to 12 years old who are exposed to air pollution related to traffic-dense areas had a higher incidence of respiratory symptoms and asthma. Children who attend school are at risk for asthma, poor attendance due

to adverse health effects, and high levels of carbon dioxide due to poor air quality and ventilation. The National Poison Data System reported that in children under 5 years old, the top 10 leading cause of poisonous deaths were analgesics, batteries, hydrocarbons, plants, cold and cough preparations, fumes/gases/vapors, pesticides, antidepressants, chemicals, and household cleaning substances (18). Though technology has benefited the cognitive development of children, the problems of living in an industrialized modern society often outweigh the benefits. For example, the need for vitamin D, the "sunshine vitamin," is "vital for the formation and maintenance of healthy bones in children, adults and infants" (19, p. 27). As we have been discussing the issues of pollution, you might take a moment to reflect upon children's rights: parents, policymakers, and corporations in the food and fuel industry all have a responsibility to provide an environment where children can thrive and grow into healthy adults (20).

> *For many children, dinner is served from a bag rushing between organized activities or sitting in front of a television. The meal itself composed a piece of meat sandwiched between two pieces of white bread and French fries filled with saturated and trans fats that complete the meal. The meal is washed down with a sweetened high fructose corn syrup drink only to return to their activities on the computer or in front of the television to have a snack of chips and soda pop. — (21, p. 433)*

As we reflect upon the dangerous effects of pollution on children, it becomes clear that children in utero throughout childhood are dependent upon us as adults to protect them and offer them the opportunity to grow into healthy adults. We have been failing them by poisoning the food, water, and air. It's time to create a life for our children where they can play in nature, drink clean water, eat food free of pesticides and chemicals, and breathe air that supports the growth of oxygenated cells. We must choose life!

**Ways to Build Strong, Healthy Children**

- Feed them organic food.
- Give them more water and drinks that are naturally flavored.
- Offer them more free-style play in the outdoors.
- Keep the home chemical-free.
- Eliminate all processed sugar and caffeine.
- Make sure they get enough sleep.
- Ask questions to assure they are happy.
- Spend more time playing and laughing with your children.
- Reduce the time spent watching television and using the computer.
- Listen to them, take their advice—they have knowledge too!
- Be mindful of their experiences and put yourself in their shoes.

Many of us are beginning to work at home, yet most of us are still spending most of our day at the worksite, often 6 to 8 hours a day. When you take the time to protect your workspace—think green—you add quality to your health.

**Solutions to Protect Your Work Environment**

- Keep the restroom sanitized by cleaning it regularly; provide adequate bath tissue, soap, and paper towels.
- Store cleaning supplies in a separate closet or cabinet from chemicals.
- Keep the office kitchen clean from dirt and garbage by having sufficient trash receptacles and emptying daily.
- Clean out refrigerators weekly.
- Discourage staff from eating at their desks.
- Look for water leakage and mold.
- Keep a friendly attitude without judgment or harassment.
- Encourage more people to use public transportation by offering free bus and light rail travel.
- Bring a healthy lunch to work.
- Eat with a friend.
- Enjoy favorable conversations versus complaining.
- Healthy attitudes make work fun.
- Take pride in your work.

**Solutions to Protect Your Community**

- Choose a fuel-efficient vehicle for yourself and encourage public transportation to replace old buses with new ones that run on cleaner fuel.
- Keep your engine tuned up and your tires inflated.
- Drive less and carpool more.
- Choose renewable energy from wind, solar, and other clean sources.
- Keep piles of papers off the floor to prevent fire.
- Create more bicycle trails; plant more trees to increase shade and absorb carbon dioxide.
- Maintain parks and forests.
- Protect parks and forests from developers by getting involved in preservation activities.
- Replace old public lighting with energy-efficient compact fluorescent light bulbs, thus reducing carbon dioxide emissions.

Now that we have discussed the issues and some of the solutions, you can begin to increase the quality of your health while living on a planet that was created to serve you. Our planet earth offers you the opportunity to breathe clean air, with vegetation emitting oxygen, and provides clean water to nourish your body. Sustain these blessings and live a long and health

## *Life Design Environment Checklist*

Things I need to do to check the air quality in my home:

___

___

___

Things I need to do to check the air quality in my workplace:

___

___

___

I know that the quality of the water I'm drinking is safe because . . .

___

___

___

I have walked through my house and have found:

___

___

___

### My Three Strategies

What I am willing to do today to be successful in creating change in my environment:

1. ___

___

___

2. ________________________________________

3. ________________________________________

### Designer Activities

*(These **activities** will help you achieve your **strategies.**)*

1. Go through all of the cabinets in your kitchen and pantry and take out everything that has chemicals or preservatives in it and write them all down. Then look up each of those chemicals and preservatives.
2. Take a dry white cotton cloth and swipe along your washer and dryer, stove, countertops, ceiling fans, patio door, window ledges, baseboards, and air conditioning ducts. Now crawl on your floors, and if by chance you have a carpet, run your fingers through it and see what comes up.
3. Take two glasses and fill one up with tap water and one with reverse-osmosis-filtered or bottled water. Switch glasses around and, without looking, choose one and explore the taste; then taste the other. Notice any differences.
4. Soften your skin: Microwave or oven-warm a small bowl of olive oil. Kick back and soak your hands. Add some granulated sugar and scrub away the extra layer of dry skin that can accumulates over time.
5. Try an invigorating hand wash: Place a tiny bit of powdered ground mustard in a bowl with some other herbs and essential oils, such as rosemary and thyme or lavender and mint. Add hot water and wait for the tingling sensation of mustard to warm your skin.

## REFLECTIVE JOURNAL

## Reference


(1) Cornell University. (2007, August 14). Pollution causes 40 percent of death world wide, study finds. *Science Daily.* Retrieved April 10, 2011, from http://www.sciencedaily.com/releases/2007/08/07081362438.htm

(2) Harper, H. A., Rodwell, V. W., & Mayes, P. A. (1977). *Review of physiological chemistry* (16th ed.). Los Altos, CA: Lange Medical Publications.

(3) Environmental Performance Report. (2001). Retrieved from http://www.tc.gc.ca/programs/environment/ems/epr2001/awareness.htm

(4) Buttram, H. (2002). An appeal for clean air in the workplace: A Review of medical-legal issues surrounding the multiple chemical sensitivity syndromes. *Townsend Letter for doctors and Patients.* August–September.

(5) *www.ewg.org Environmental Working Group.*

(6) Orben, R. (2001). *Environ Health Perspectives, 109,* 145–501

(7) 40. http://www.infrared-sauna-reference.com

(8) Ealy, H. (in press). *The greatest energy always prevails. Volume 1: Interesting insights into advanced natural medicine.*

(9) Environmental Protection Agency. (2007).

(10) http://www.msnbc.msn.com/id/23558785

(11) http://www.energysavers.gov/your_home/water_heating/index.cfm/mytopic513090r

(12) (http://www.fmi,org/docs/media/bg/pests.pdf).

(13) Ries, N. M., Rachul, C., & Caulfield, T. (2011). Newspaper reporting on legislative and policy interventions to address obesity: United States, Canada, and the United Kingdom. *Journal of Public Health Policy, 32,* 73–90.

(14) Louv, R. (2007, March/April). Leave no child inside. *Orion Magazine.*

(15) Bronstein, A., Spyker, C., Cantilena, D. A., Green, L. R. M., Rumack, J. L., & Giffin, B. H. (2010). Annual Report of the American Association of Poison Control Centers' National Poison Data System (NPDS): 27th Annual Report. *Clinical Toxicology, 48*(10), 979–1178.

(16) Kalro, B. N. (2009, April). Vitamin D and the skeleton. *Alternative Therapies in Women's Health, 11*(4), 25–32.

(17) Purcell, M. (2010) Raising healthy children: Moral and political responsibility for childhood obesity. *Journal of Public Health Policy, 31*(4), 433–446.

(18) Environ Health Perspectives. (2001) 109: 145–501.

# CHAPTER 3

© Bedolaga, 2011. Used under license from Shutterstock, Inc.

# Healthful Eating

*Tell me what you eat, I'll tell you who you are.*

*~Anthelme Brillat-Savarin*

We all have our own way of doing things. It is amazing how we act out of habit and how difficult it is to change these habits. Eating and your diet are habits learned through life experience. You learned which foods you "love," whether they are healthy and nutritious or not. These "love" foods typically come from childhood experiences. Some of us also enjoy foods that have ethnic origins. Others eat foods that are easy to purchase and access, such as fast foods. Remember the film *Super Size Me*. The message was that overdoing one type of food—easy to obtain and quick to eat—was physically dangerous! Some of us also have comfort foods that we are drawn to, such as cookies or chocolate, or perhaps there are certain foods that have particular memories, both good and not so good.

Regardless of your choices, the food you put into your body is metabolized in specific ways. Metabolism, the way food is digested and used, is dependent on genetics and also on how foods are organically used by body systems designed for food consumption, use, and elimination.

You may be familiar with the different food groups that are organized as dietary guidelines. Further information about recommended daily allowances of the five main food groups (vegetables, fruits, grains, lean meats and beans, milk, and oil) can be found at http://www.nutrition.gov. These food groups are essential in providing appropriate and adequate nourishment for your body. They are not to be taken lightly, as these foods are what your body needs to function at its optimal level. For children, eating the correct amounts of foods from these groups is an absolute requirement for "normal" growth and development. In addition, the amount of calories (units of food energy) you need changes depending on age, body type, activity, and life space (such as pregnancy, chronic conditions, etc.).

The best way to eat healthfully is to do just that. Of course this is easy to say but often difficult due to your lifestyle, financial resources, access to healthy foods, and your responsibilities. In *Dietary Guidelines for Americans 2010* (1) it was found that Americans were not eating enough whole grains, vegetables, fruits, dairy products,

> **The Obesity Epidemic**
>
> More than one-third of U.S. adults—more than 72 million people—and 17% of U.S. children are obese. From 1980 through 2008, obesity rates for adults have doubled and rates for children have tripled. During the past several decades, obesity rates for all groups in society, regardless of age, sex, race, ethnicity, socioeconomic status, education level, or geographic region, have increased markedly (2).

and fiber, and also did not get enough vitamin D, potassium, and calcium from their diets. They were also ingesting too many solid fats and added sugar calories, refined grains, sodium, and saturated fat.

The simple fact is that awareness and recognition of what it takes to eat nutritiously is not as demanding as having to deal with being over- or underweight or living with chronic conditions resulting from a lifetime of unwise eating patterns and habits. If you have children, start them early in understanding and becoming familiar and comfortable with eating foods that are "good for them." Interestingly, if your children are eating well, so can you. Become a role model and an exemplar of good eating habits. You can choose to eat well. Unfortunately, if you don't, the consequences are daunting.

Being overweight or obese is a challenge in the United States. The statistics are astounding. Obesity is defined as a body mass index (BMI) of 30 or greater. BMI is calculated from a person's weight and height and degree of body fatness. Over the last 20 years, there has been a dramatic increase in obesity in the United States (3).

*The belly rules the mind.*

~*Spanish proverb*

Dieting has become a way of life for many who are or who perceive themselves to be "not at the right weight." These range from simple diets constructed by one's own desires and imagination to diets purchased either by buying a book, going to classes and seminars, and/or purchasing specific food provided under the diet's requirements. There are so many opportunities to try a different diet that for some it seems overwhelming to even begin. Others take a buffet approach and try some or many different diets. The bottom line on dieting is that no matter what approach you take, you must always be aware that your body must be nourished with appropriate combinations of protein, carbohydrates, and fats. The most important part of dieting is to not do it alone. Consult a healthcare provider about what type of diet may work best for you, particularly if you have a chronic illness or condition.

Deciding on the "right" diet is essential. For weight loss, there are several essential elements. You must determine the number of calories that is right for you, and weight loss should be no more than one pound per week. The diet should contain good nutrition, meaning the following (4):

- There are adequate vitamins and minerals.
- There is adequate protein—the average woman (25 years old) should get 50 grams of protein a day and the average man at that same age should get 63 grams.
- There is an adequate amount of carbohydrates—at least 100 grams.
- Intake of fiber is 20 to 30 grams.
- No more than 30 percent of calories is from fat.

Dieting as a lifestyle pattern is often seen as temporary and is either not sustained or does not achieve what was intended. The outcome for many who are not successful in eating nutritiously or who do not reach their diet goals is being overweight or obese.

There are many diets available, from fixed-menu to exchange, to pre-packaged to formula and flexible diets. A study conducted in May 2009, identified the most popular diets today (5). The criteria used for selection included the number of articles found about the diet, how popular the diet seemed to be, and the feedback received on the individual diet. The following are the diets found to meet these criteria:

| **Diet** | **Description** |
|---|---|
| Atkins | Low carbohydrate intake to burn stored body fat. |
| The Zone | Aim for a nutritional balance of 40% carbohydrates, 30% fats, and 30% proteins at every meal. Encourages the consumption of good-quality carbohydrates. |
| Vegetarian | The majority of vegetarians are lacto-ovo vegetarian, which means they do not eat animal-based foods except for eggs, dairy, and honey. |
| Vegan | Considered a way of life. Nothing animal based, including eggs, dairy, and honey. |
| Weight Watchers | Lose weight through diet, exercise, and a support network. |
| South Beach | Control of insulin. Focus on the benefits of unrefined slow carbohydrates rather than fast carbohydrates. |
| Raw Food | Consuming foods and drinks that are not processed, are completely plant based, and ideally are organic. |
| Mediterranean | Focus on plant foods, fresh fruits as dessert, beans, nuts, cereals, seeds, and olive oil as the main source of fat. Cheese and yogurt are the main dairy, and fish, poultry, and eggs (limited) with small amounts of lean meat comprise the protein. |

(6, 7, 8, 9, 10)

Damage from excess weight is massive, from dealing with one's body image to organic and chronic disorders such as diabetes. Many have gone to more extreme measures to deal with their weight by using surgical procedures as a way to quickly provide an intervention. Often these individuals have tried many other means and found that losing weight by dieting and exercise was not successful. Often, associated illnesses due to being overweight motivated the surgery. You have most likely seen or read about many success stories and, sadly, failures using this approach; however, it has become a recognized part of the healthcare industry and is called bariatrics.

On the other side of the food coin are those who are obsessed with their weight. Their body image may be distorted and there may be shame or anxiety about body size and shape. Many are diagnosed with anorexia nervosa (self-starvation) or binge-eating disorder (bulimia nervosa, binging and purging).

© CROX, 2011. Used under license from Shutterstock, Inc.

These dysfunctional strategies become ways to deal with body image perceptions and are considered eating disorders.

Another important aspect of nourishing your being is your fluid intake. Fifty-five to 60% of body weight is water. We can lose quite a bit of water by breathing, sweating, and through elimination. Staying hydrated (having enough fluids in your body daily) is essential, especially if you live in an arid, hot climate and if you exercise routinely. It is said that one must drink "8 glasses of water" daily or, using another standard, half of your body weight in fluid ounces daily. You may ask, what does this mean and why do it? Do you only drink water and, if so, what type of water? Can you drink other fluids, and which ones have the greatest value? And, finally, what is the best way to consume all of this fluid?

The obvious benefits of hydration include increases in energy, and with adequate hydration you increase your mood and foster clarity in thinking. Even the smallest amount of dehydration can slow the body down significantly and cause changes in the cardiovascular, thermoregulatory, metabolic, and central nervous systems.

Daily fluid intake can be from all beverages and foods. Fruits and vegetables contain water and drinks, especially those that are not caffeinated, are a good source as well. Herbal teas and freshly made vegetable and fruit juices are excellent. The temperature of the fluid has some impact. Hot, lukewarm, or cold fluids will have different effects on your body. For example, lukewarm fluid does not have the same drastic impact as hot or cold fluid as your body does not have to work as hard to respond. Alternating fluid temperatures is recommended, as is drinking your largest amount of fluid two hours before and after meals (11).

If you do drink water, take care in the type of water you select. If you are drinking tap water, you are likely consuming "reclaimed and treated" water, which may contain various amounts of lead, aluminum, bacteria, viruses, and pesticides. Bottled or filtered water is one way to ensure you are drinking "cleaner" water (11).

One simple way to determine hydration is to check your urine. If it is pale yellow you are adequately hydrated. If the color becomes darker and concentrated, this is your signal to drink more.

© Pakhnyushcha, 2011. Used under license from Shutterstock, Inc.

Vitamins and dietary supplements as well as herbal remedies have become popular ways to also improve nutrition. They are easy to access from providers of healthcare and are equally as simple to purchase in retail or specialty stores. You can even order them via television, the Internet, or from advertisements in a variety of print publications. There are so many different ones that it can become confusing as to which are appropriate and effective. Further, you must consider which ones you can take given your body type, size, and what prescription medication or other supplements you are taking.

Vitamins and minerals are fairly easy to determine, as they are contained in the food you eat and Recommended Dietary Allowances (RDAs) have been researched for years. You can find more information on vitamins by linking to http://www.nutrition.org

Dietary supplements are more challenging to make decisions about, as they have become popular and accepted in our culture. They are touted as being incredibly helpful for nearly every disease and condition. Taking care when selecting supplements is as important as the care you take in the type of dietary regime you select.

Remember that the foods entering your mouth are a decision you make on a daily, minute-by-minute basis. Becoming aware of what you eat, how you eat, where you eat, and when you eat is critical to becoming "healthy." The amount of food you eat impacts your metabolism, so that fasting or entering into the world of anorexia or bulimia as a way to control food intake is dangerous. Equally dangerous is the timing of when you eat. Fasting is not particularly kind to your body. Your body craves food on an ongoing basis.

Eating in front of the television, when standing at a counter, or even gobbling food while driving are not the best venues for digestion. Just ask those who face a lifetime of acid reflux now commonly known as GERD. So be mindful in selecting your particular "brand" of nutrition and manner of eating. Doing this will surely lead you to the healthful eating that is the foundation of a quality life.

## Life Design Healthful Eating Checklist

Reflect on the following to evaluate the extent to which you are currently eating nutritiously and getting enough fluids to be sufficiently hydrated.

What foods do you like the most/the least?

______________________________________________

______________________________________________

______________________________________________

What foods have memories for you? Describe the foods and associated memories.

______________________________________________

______________________________________________

______________________________________________

What snacks do you eat on a daily basis? When do you eat those snacks? Are they nutritious snacks or ones that have "empty" calories?

______________________________________________

______________________________________________

______________________________________________

How much water do you drink daily? List what you typically drink in a day and calculate and list that in number of 8-ounce glasses.

______________________________________________

______________________________________________

______________________________________________

What vitamins/supplements do you take on a regular basis? In what ways do they help your nutrition?

______________________________________________

______________________________________________

______________________________________________

If you have been on a diet recently, identify the diet you were on. Was the diet successful or not successful and in what ways?

______________________________________________________________________

______________________________________________________________________

______________________________________________________________________

## My Three Strategies

**What I am willing to do today to eat healthfully and be sufficiently hydrated:**

1. ______________________________________________________________________
______________________________________________________________________
2. ______________________________________________________________________
______________________________________________________________________
3. ______________________________________________________________________
______________________________________________________________________

## Designer Activities

*(These **activities** will help you achieve your **strategies**.)*

- Look at yourself in the mirror. Decide from your own perspective: Are you overweight, underweight, or just at the right weight? As a matter of reference, look at what weight is considered appropriate for your height and body type. Identify some action steps, if appropriate.
- Start a diary or list of what you eat each day. Be honest by identifying everything that enters your mouth. Do this for a week and then evaluate if you are eating all food groups and recommended allowances. Set goals if you believe you need to make any changes to your diet.
- If you are on a diet, assess whether the diet is providing you with adequate nutrition. If not, set goals to make changes.
- Purchase a small notebook and write down how much you drink each day. List what you drink in estimated ounces. Add it up daily and then look at how much and what you have had to drink. Create this list for one week. At the end of the week examine your list and calculations. If you are not getting enough to drink, add different types of fluids and increase their amount.
- Look at the vitamins and/or supplements you are taking. Write a short description of each by doing research on them. Link them to the food you eat and set goals if you believe a change is needed. You may also want to talk with a healthcare provider about what you are taking and the impact it may have on any prescribed medications.
- Think about the last time you went to a restaurant. What foods did you select and eat? Were they nutritious? If not, what foods might you have eaten that would have been better nourishment for your body?

# Your Healthful Eating
## REFLECTIVE JOURNAL

*Take the time now to write down your "real" intention for change. Use this journal to describe the ways you will be sure you eat healthfully, selecting foods that are nutritious. Include ways you can increase your fluid intake. Don't forget to list any barriers and how you will overcome them.*

## Reference

(1) Center for Disease Control and Prevention. (2010). Building healthy eating patterns. In *Dietary Guidelines for Americans, 2010*. Retrieved from http://www.cdc.gov

(2) Centers for Disease Control and Prevention (CDC). (2010). Obesity: Halting the epidemic making health crisis: At a glance 2010. Retrieved from http:www.cdc.gov

(3) Centers for Disease Control and Prevention (CDC). (2010). US obesity trends 1985–2009. Retrieved from http://www.cdc.gov

(4) Healthy Weight Forum. (2010). Choosing the right diet. Retrieved from http://www.healthweightforum.org

(5) Medical News Today. (2009). What are the eight most popular diets today? Retrieved from http://www.medicalnewstoday.com

(6) Baker, B. (2006). Weight loss and diet plans: Several types of diet plans produce at least short-term weight loss: Portion size may matter more than what we eat. *American Journal of Nursing, 10*(6), 52–59.

(7) Futternan, R. (2006). Comparison of the Atkins, Ornish, Weight Watchers, and Zone diets for weight loss and heart disease reduction. *American Journal of Health Promotion, 20*(3), 228–229.

(8) Malik, V. S. (2007). Popular weight-loss diets: From evidence to practice. *Nature Clinical Practice Cardiovascular Medicine, 4*(1), 34–41.

(9) Rayokowski, L. K. (2006). Popular diets: What practitioners should know. *Nurse Practitioner, 31*(10), 55–57.

(10) Volpe, S. L. (2006). Popular weight reduction diets. *Journal of Cardiovascular Nursing, 21*(1), 34–39.

(11) Henele, Dr. (2011). The greatest energy always prevails. Vol. 1: *Interesting insights into advanced natural medicine*. Tempe, AZ: No Limit Publishing Group.

## Other Readings to Explore

Bauer, J. (2005). *Total nutrition*. New York: Penguin Group.

Blackburn, G., & Corliss, J. (2008). *Break through your set point: How to finally lose the weight you want and keep it off*. New York: William Morrow.

Foley, D. (2007, July). 12-eat right diet rules that work. *Prevention.*

French, S. A., Story, M., & Jeffery, R. W. (2001). Environmental influences on eating and physical activity. *Annual Review of Public Health, 22*, 309–335.

Greenwald, A. (2006). Current nutritional treatments of obesity. *Advances in Psychosomatic Medicine, 27*, 24–41.

Haas, E. M. (2006). *Staying healthy with nutrition*. Berkeley, CA: Celestial Arts.

Hendel, G. (2003). *Water & salt*. Natural Resources.

Latest nutrients report card shows some failing grades. (2006, January). *Tufts University Health & Nutrition Newsletter, 23*(11), 8.

National Institutes of Mental Health. (2007). Eating disorders. Retrieved from http://www.nimh.nih.gov/health/publications/eating-disorders/summary.shtml

O'Keefe, J. H. (2008). Nutrition 101: Physicians can no longer ignore the healing power of diet and nutritional supplements. *Expert Review of Cardiovascular Therapy, 6*(5), 593–596.

Sadovsky, R., Collins, N., Tighe, A. P., Brunton, S. A., & Safeer, R. (2008). Patient use of dietary supplements: A clinician's perspective. *Current Medical Research and Opinion, 24*(4), 1209–1216.

Scholar, G. (2007). You deserve a health lifestyle. *American Nursing Today, 2*, 28–30.

Sharpe, P. A., Blanck, H. M., Williams, J. E., Ainsworth, B. E., & Conway, J. M. (2007). Use of complementary and alternative medicine for weight control in the United States. *Journal of Alternative and Complementary Medicine, 13*(2), 217–222.

Taubes, G. (2009). *Good calories, bad calories: Fats, carbs, and the controversial science of diet and health.* New York: Anchor.

The facts of five diet myths. (2006, July). *Tufts University Health & Nutrition Newsletter, 24*(5), 5.

Vasey, C. (2006). *The water prescription*. Healing Arts Press.

CHAPTER 4

# My Body, My Strength

*Fear less, hope more; Eat less, chew more; Whine less, breathe more; Talk less, say more; Love more, and all good things will be yours.*

*~Swedish Proverb*

There are mirrors everywhere! Some mirrors reflect what you actually look like to yourself and to others. These mirrors reveal what you "see" as your reflected body image. The mirror may show a true reality or what you perceive your reality to be, the way you see yourself. Sometimes you are perfectly happy with your image and other times you wish it was different. Different may be your longing to be shorter or taller, thinner or fatter, prettier, or even more confident in the way you handle your affairs.

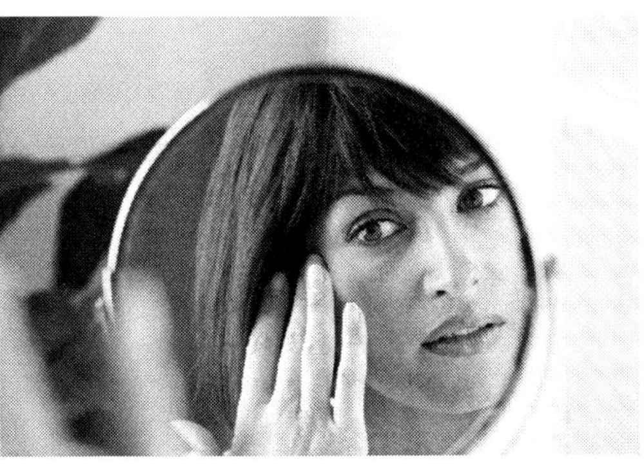



Body image is related to your developmental messages and the creation of your self-esteem. But no matter how you perceive yourself, whether it reflects reality or not, the image you have affects the actions and decisions you make in your everyday life. You think about your body image with every step you take, whether it is a conscious or subconscious act. Your image even shadows the life decisions you make, such as what career you are capable of, whom you may have a relationship with, even down to the clothes you buy, the car you select, the house you live in, and the food you buy.

You may wonder what influences your body image. For one, the media, both written and broadcast, play a large role. The next time you are at a food market or drugstore, go to the magazine shelf. Scan the magazines that relate to fashion, beauty, or even family lifestyle. What you will see are images of very attractive, thin, and fit men and women. Even the men and women who are older also reflect this same image. Certainly "models" have always had the stereotype of being extremely thin, often emaciated. Thankfully, in the recent past and currently, the fashion industry is beginning to be more aware that "normal" individuals cannot and are not able to maintain such a body structure. From a business and marketing perspective, we are now starting to see models whose attributes are "curvier."

Body image also emanates from the messages you received as a child and the significant others you lived with. If fitness and exercise were thought to be important and a conscious part of your growing up, you will likely maintain that as an adult and see yourself as someone who is active and who wants to be fit. As an adult, if your partner or friends are involved in exercise or sports activities, you will likely want to actively participate, even if your goal is more social than physical.

Will a positive body image make a difference? Will you be more happy and adjusted, and find more joy in your life? It won't hurt. However, remember that your body image must be realistic. You need to work with what you have. Try not to compare yourself with others and stop those negative thoughts if you don't match up. Rather, celebrate and nurture what you have. Find the joy in what you can do and invest in yourself.

Let's get started. There are certain body types that have been identified as body "models," and these are often helpful in determining your type:

- The Ectomorph—Ectomorphs have a thin build with little muscle and fat. They have difficulty gaining weight. This body type is not able to manage high amounts of athletic training. Ectomorphs have a higher metabolism that keeps fat levels in check.
- The Endomorph—Endomorphs have a large round body with high levels of fat and more muscle density. They have trouble losing weight but an easier time gaining muscle as well as fat.
- The Mesomorph—Mesomorphs are very athletic with a muscular frame that has relatively low amounts of body fat. They don't have trouble losing fat and easily gain muscle. They have a higher metabolism that keeps fat levels in check.

What does body type have to do with strength? It helps you think through the kinds of activities that fit your body type, allowing you to design a more specific active lifestyle that can align with proper exercise.

Exercise and activity come in many forms, from training for a sport to going to a gym to work out, to even doing work on your house. Unfortunately, in the United States, we have become more sedentary than active. The American Heart Association (1) has reported that 70% of Americans do not achieve their recommended levels of physical activity, which is moderate-intensity aerobic exercise for 30 minutes five days a week. If you haven't been exercising, physical exercise guidelines recommend that adults should start off by exercising three or more times a week for 20 minutes or more and then go to 30 minutes, four to six times a week (2). Basic recommendations from the American College of Sports Medicine and the American Heart Association (3) include moderate cardio 30 minutes a day, five days a week (as cited above) or vigorous intense cardio 20 minutes a day, three days a week and 8 to 10 strength-training exercises, with 8 to 12 repetitions of each exercise, twice a week.

Just as with weight, exercise and active lifestyles require thought and then action. If you are already exercising, is it the "right" exercise for you? Is it adding to the strength of your body or is it just a ritual that has become habit forming? Remember that the endorphins secreted during exercise give you a "personal high" but may not be adding to the strength quotient you would like to achieve. If you are not exercising at all, what is keeping you from adding this to your "personal life design"?

© Mircea BEZERGHEANU, 2011. Used under license from Shutterstock, Inc.

Determining the best way to exercise may take some research and perhaps consultation. For some, exercising at home with a prescribed routine works well. Others seek personal trainers who provide more discipline and focused activity. Even others find going to a gym the best way to fortify their body and perhaps it also takes care of social needs. And yet others use sports or recreational activities, such as running or cycling, as their best "fit." Whatever it is, your body needs routine exercise.

There are different types of exercise. Flexibility exercise includes stretching, which improves your range of muscle and joint motion. Aerobic exercise includes walking, cycling, hiking, running, and playing tennis, which focus on increasing endurance. Anaerobic exercise includes weight training, increasing short-term muscle strength, and conditioning (4). Moderate physical activities include walking briskly (about 3.5 miles per hour), hiking, gardening, dancing, and a general light workout with weights contrasted with vigorous physical activities such as running/jogging (5 miles per hour), bicycling, swimming (free-style laps), and heavy yard work (5).

Following is a summary of different types of exercise that may be useful in your research to determine what might be right for your body and lifestyle:

| Type of Exercise | Impact on the Body | Types |
|---|---|---|
| Aerobic | 3–5 times a week | Walking, running, biking, swimming, skating, stair climbing, rowing, aerobic classes |
| Muscle Conditioning | 2–3 times a week | Weight training, free weights, weight machines, circuit/interval workouts |
| Routine Activities | Daily | Housecleaning, car washing, window cleaning, painting, gardening |

There are other forms of exercise that may be helpful. Movement therapy, for example, incorporates mind-body practices and focuses on the interaction between the brain, mind, body, and behavior, with the intent to use the mind to affect physical functioning to promote health. The complementary and alternative medicine modalities that relate to movement are as follows (6):

| Type of Movement Therapy | Description |
|---|---|
| **YOGA** | Combines physical postures, breathing techniques, and meditation or relaxation. People use yoga as part of a general health regimen, and also for a variety of health conditions. Different types of yoga include hatha, vinyasa, ashtanga and power, and bikram/hot. Performed in classes once a week or more for 45 minutes. |
| **PILATES** | Uses physical exercise to strengthen and build control of muscles, especially those used for posture. Awareness of breathing and precise control of movements are essential. |

*(Continued)*

| Type of Movement Therapy | Description |
|---|---|
| **QI GONG** | Use of gentle physical movements, mental focus, and deep breathing directed toward specific parts of the body. Performed in repetition. Two or more times a week for 30 minutes. |
| **TAI CHI** | Movement of the body slowly and gently while breathing deeply and meditating. Movements are called routines. |

Several mind-body approaches ranked among the top 10 complementary and alternative medicine (CAM) practices reported by adults (7). The survey found that 12.7% of adults had used deep-breathing exercises, 9.4% had practiced meditation, and 6.1% had practiced yoga; use of these three CAM practices had increased significantly since the previous survey in 2002.

Whatever exercise you select, it is essential that you do something. One way to get started is to identify what "fitness" goals you have and what life barriers may be preventing you from getting started.

**Setting Your Fitness Goals (8)**

List two long-term fitness goals. Be specific, such as "I want to exercise 30 minutes five times a week."

1.
2.

List two *short-term* goals *per* each long-term goal. For example, "By March 1 I will exercise 20 minutes three times a week."

1.
2.

What are the barriers to exercising? Check all that apply.

| | | |
|---|---|---|
| No time | Too tired | Inconvenient |
| Can't find time | Don't want to be sore | Uncomfortable |
| Easily discouraged | Family obligations | Apprehensive |
| Lack of discipline | Work obligations | Don't see value |
| Failed in the past | Don't want to sweat | Boring |

Other(s): ______________________________________

Of the barriers checked, pick your two greatest barriers and write a possible solution for the barrier.

1. ______________________________Barrier

Solution:

2. ______________________________Barrier

Solution:

Unquestionably, exercise has many benefits, such as maintaining healthy weight, building bone density, increasing muscle strength and mobility, combating chronic disease, improving your mood and sleep, and strengthening your immune system. Be careful, though. Do not over-exercise. It can be harmful. The body needs at least a day of rest, which is why it is suggested that you start by exercising only three days a week (9). Also take care that you do not become a "weekend warrior" and intensify your exercise only on the weekend when you have the time.

The President's Council on Physical Fitness and Sports (10) provides some helpful guidelines for commitment to a personal exercise program. The first and probably most important is to have patience and give exercise a chance. Allow yourself to rejoice in the experience of improved fitness and feeling better. It is suggested that you warm up for about 5 to 10 minutes and then alternate your time between muscular strength and endurance, cardio-respiratory endurance, and flexibility exercise. A cool-down is also suggested for 5 to 10 minutes. The time to exercise tends to be early in the morning for some, as they feel that it makes them more focused and gives them much more energy on the job. Other individuals exercise at night because they like the change of pace from the busy work day, and exercise relieves them from the build-up of tension and anxiety.

As you work on your fitness and exercise plan, beware of the "muscle hustle"—the companies who try to sell you exercise equipment. The Federal Trade Commission (11) offers some advice. Be skeptical of testimonials. What works for one person may not work for another. Ignore claims that the equipment can provide long lasting, easy, "no sweat" results. You must exercise to get the benefits of exercise. Also, be sure of what you are buying, Read the small print, get warranties and return policies, and ask if there is technical and customer support.

Staying motivated is the key. Be sure you set goals, make exercise a part of your life plan, track your progress, and, if you can, exercise with a friend or colleague. Most of all, be flexible, stay on track, and have fun (12)!

Getting started today on a route to fitness can only improve the quality of your life. What a high to look in the mirror and see the results of just spending 2% of the 1,440 minutes you have each day!

### *Life Design Exercise Checklist*

Reflect on the following to evaluate the extent to which you are currently exercising.

How would you describe your body image? Use words or even draw a picture that would best describe what your body looks like to you. To others?

______________________________________________

______________________________________________

______________________________________________

What type(s) of exercise do you currently participate in each week?

______________________________________________

______________________________________________

______________________________________________

How much time to you devote to exercise each week?

______________________________________________

______________________________________________

______________________________________________

How do you feel before and after exercising of any kind? Share your thoughts and feelings.

______________________________________________

______________________________________________

______________________________________________

**My Three Strategies**

What I am willing to do today to start my fitness plan and be successful in exercising regularly:

1. ______________________________________________

   ______________________________________________

2. ______________________________________________
______________________________________________

3. ______________________________________________
______________________________________________

**Designer Activities**

*(These **activities** will help you achieve your **strategies.**)*

- If you already have an active fitness/exercise plan, keep a journal of what you do, how often you do it, and how you feel during and after exercising. Describe what keeps you exercising so you can remember that when you don't want to exercise.
- If you are not exercising at all, list the types of exercises you would like to do and then list what keeps you from doing them. Then describe ways in which you can decrease these potential barriers so you can start a fitness/exercise plan. Be sure to start with small, realistic goals.
- If you know any individuals who have been successful with a fitness/exercise plan, interview them and find out what motivated them to start and what keeps them "on track."
- If you are not able to actively exercise due to a chronic or debilitating condition, describe ways in which you can keep your body strong.

# Strengthening My Body

## REFLECTIVE JOURNAL

*As you think about exercise and fitness, take time to write down your "real" intention for change. Use this Reflective Journal to describe the ways you will more fully integrate the changes you want to make. Don't forget to list any barriers you may encounter and how you will overcome them.*

## Reference

(1) American Heart Association. (2011). Physical activity. Retrieved from http://www.heart.org/HEARTORG/GettingHealthy/PhysicalActivity/Physical-Activity_UCM_001080_SubHomePage.jsp

(2) Familydoctor.org. (2006). Exercise: How to get started. American Academy of Family Physicians. Retrieved from http://familydoctor.org/onlin/famdocen/home/healthy/physical/basics/015.printerview.html

(3) American Heart Association and American College of Sports Medicine. (2007). Physical activity and public health guidelines. Retrieved from http://www.acsm.org/AM/Template.cfm?Section+Home_Page &TEMPLATE=/CM/HTMLDisplay.cfm

(4) PreventDisease.com. (2008). Modes of fitness, aerobic, anaerobic. Retrieved from http://www.preventdisease.com/fitness/fundament/articles/modesfitness.html

(5) United States Department of Agriculture (USDA). (2011). What is physical activity? Retrieved from http://www.mypyramid.gov

(6) National Institutes of Health. National Center for Complementary and Alternative Medicine. (2011). Get the facts. Retrieved from http://nccam.nih.gov

(7) Centers for Disease Control and Prevention. (2007). National Health Interview Survey. Retrieved from http://www.cdc.gov/nchs/nhis.htm

(8) Burke, J. (2008). *Goals and barriers worksheet*. Phoenix: Body Definitions, LLC.

(9) MayoClinic.com. (2008). Exercise: 7 benefits of regular physical activity. Retrieved from http://www.mayoclinic.com/print/exercise/HQ01676/METHOD=print.

(10) The President's Council on Physical Fitness and Sports. (2008). Fitness fundamentals: Guidelines for personal exercise programs. Retrieved from http://www.fitness.gov/fitness.htm

(11) Federal Trade Commission. (2003). Avoiding the muscle hustle: Tips for buying exercise equipment. Retrieved from http://www.ftc.gov/bcp/online/pubs/alerts/musclealrt.com

(12) MayoClinic.com. (2008). Fitness programs: 10 tips for staying motivated. Retrieved from http://www.mayoclinic.com/print/fitness/HQ01543/METHOD=print

## Other Readings to Explore

Cohen, K. (1999). The way of qigong: The art and science of Chinese energy healing. New York, NY: Wellspring/Ballantine.

Exercise and physical activity for older adults. (1998). *Medicine & Science in Sports & Exercise, 30*(6). Retrieved from http://www. acsm.org.

How can you design a workout according to your body type? (2011). Retrieved from http://www.bodybuilding.com

How much exercise is enough? (2003, Winter). American College of Sports Medicine Fit Society Page. Retrieved from http://www.acsm.org

Jakicic, J. M., & Otto, A. (2006). Treatment and prevention of obesity: What is the role of exercise? *Nutrition Reviews, 64*(2), 557–561.

Li, J. (2005). The inner structure of Tai Chi: Mastering the classic forms of tai chi chi kung. Rochester, VT: Destiny Books.

Model for health body image. (2008). Retrieved from BodyImageHealth.org.

Wu, B. (2006). Qi gong for total wellness: Increase your energy, vitality, and longevity with the ancient 9 palaces system for the white cloud monastery. New York, NY: St. Martins Press.

Yang, J. (1997). The root of Chinese qigong: Secrets of health, longevity & enlightenment. Wolfeboro, NH: Ymaa Publication Center.

CHAPTER 5

© Strider, 2011. Used under license from Shutterstock, Inc.

# Rest, Relaxation, and Recreation: Restoring Balance

*Choose Life! Only that and always! At whatever risk, to let life leak out, to let it wear away by the mere passage of time, to withhold giving and spending it. . . . is to choose nothing.*

*~Sister Helen Kelly*

The discussion in this chapter will focus on the three R's: rest, relaxation, and recreation. Your daily life often consists of working, eating, shopping, caring for others, and technology stimulation, frequently taking you away from these three simple essentials. Can you honestly say that you have enough rest, relaxation, and recreation in your life? It has been estimated that 7 in 10 American adults are not regularly active during their leisure time, and 4 out of 10 are not active at all (1). If you are like most people living in a modern culture, you are probably not getting enough of the three R's. Many of us live by the golden rule that productivity "makes the person," versus play and recreation. With today's technical advancements you can produce what you could in 1948 in less than half the time. Nevertheless, free time has fallen almost 40% from a median of 26 hours per week to under 17. Research has shown that people would like to cut back on the hours they work, but the most common reason they don't is debt (2, p. 244–245). If you let go of the addiction to spending you just might have more time for rest, relaxation, and recreation, most often free commodities. A study of 10- to 17-year-olds who had cell phones found that 52% sent text messages from a movie theater; 96% communicated with their parents daily via cell phone; 28% sent messages from the dinner table; 33% would rather give up radio, video games, or trips to the mall than their cell phones; and 20% would give up television and 25% would give up their MP3 players rather than give up their cell phones (3, p. 49). On the other hand, a study of 17,000 teens that were involved in a recreation center showed 75% were more likely to engage in moderate-to-vigorous physical activity (4). In spite of the lack of time you allocate for nurturing yourself, all is not lost; let's take a look at bringing restoration back into your life.

© Hung Chung Chih, 2011. Used under license from Shutterstock, Inc.

### *Rest and Relaxation*

One way to experience rest and relaxation is to do absolutely nothing! This can be a rejuvenating experience.—Letting go of everything for a day is a great exercise to practice to fine tune your awareness. Activities that quiet the mind, such as meditation, yoga, cross-stitching, sewing, painting, beading, and playing or listening to music, are but a few ways to enjoy relaxation. Research has found that subjects' heart rates increased while engaged in yoga postures and decreased in guided relaxation and after cyclic meditation. The increase in sympathetic activation during the practice of yoga postures and increase of parasympathetic activity in cyclic meditation offers a balance of exercise and relaxation in the activities (5).

© Tatiana Popova, 2011. Used under license from Shutterstock, Inc.

Using the scent of essential oils to enhance relaxation is a delicious experience. Research has found that aromatherapy massage increased the shared attention behaviors of children with autism and severe learning disabilities, such as eye contact, pointing, and sharing experiences with others (6). There are many scents to choose from to add extra quality to your life. For example, tangerine, lavender, ylang ylang, geranium, and jasmine aid in stimulating relaxation. You can use them in a diffuser, in your bath, or dab a small amount on your forehead or behind your ears. Following are some of the benefits to your body when you give it sufficient rest and relaxation.

**Benefits of Rest and Relaxation**

- Resting and relaxing "recharges your batteries" by generating energy that you can later use for work or play.
- Getting enough sleep (eight to nine hours a night) improves learning and memory, stabilizes metabolism and weight, increases safety from accidents due to sleepiness, and maintains decreased stress hormone levels and normal heartbeat while improving immune function (7).
- Clearing your mind from the various "mindless monsters" that dictate the "shoulds and have to 's" offers your mind a rest from thoughts that consume you on a daily basis. As a result, you feel less anxious and distracted and experience more joy and focus.
- Finding ways to explore your creativity unleashes positive energy and establishes more of a connection to your inner self.

© Leah-Anne Thompson, 2011. Used under license from Shutterstock, Inc.

Of course, getting enough sleep is vital for maintaining good health. Sleep is as important to good health as oxygen. Your nervous system depends upon you getting enough sleep to work properly. Surprisingly, even a slight deprivation of a night's sleep can negatively affect one's health. A well-known study showed that rats that who were sleep deprived died within three weeks (8). If you sleep well you open up the opportunity to feel invigorated and rejuvenated to begin your day.

### Recreation

Let's turn our attention to the benefits of recreation. How much time do you spend "playing" and indulging in leisure activities? How often do you connect with nature and enjoy the interchange of energies? Recreation improves our quality of life by increasing self-esteem, (9) self-sufficiency, connection to others, and mental clarity (10), and reduces anxiety and stress 2003 (11). In young adults, recreation also serves to help prevent juvenile crime, underage drinking, and illegal drug use, and helps to improve academic performance (12). Teens who do not engage in after-school activities are five times more likely to be "D" students than those who do participate (13). Youth who participate in recreation activities explore strategies for problem solving, play fair, plan, and enhance motor skills (14). Research shows that a window view of nature (rather than a building environment) increases recovery from surgery, and results in less use of healthcare services among prison inmates, improves work performance in job settings, and increases job satisfaction (15). These benefits relate to having a view of nature through a window! Can you imagine the benefits if you participate in activities in nature? How you engage in leisure is equally important to the time spent in leisure activities.

Research has found that physical activity actually promotes the growth of brain cells in the part of the brain that controls memory and learning. This proves that brain cells can be replaced (16, p. 26), One wonders if you would see a decrease in Alzheimer's disease if elders were more active beginning in their earlier years and throughout the golden years. In one study, more time engaged in physically active activities was associated with higher levels of health (17, p. 73). What happened to the childhood days of playing and walking in the park? You did not think about the benefits; it was a part of life to be in nature. The benefits are still there, yet you need to take advantage of them. It has been found that people who visit parks and engage in recreation report fewer visits to a physician for purposes other than wellness checks than do non-park users, and that depression was reduced by the size of someone's social network, level of physical activity, and interaction with friends during park and recreation activities (18). Adding time in your daily activities for rest, relaxation, and recreation will incrementally pay off. Think about how important it is to be happy, free spirited, and just let go!

How you show up for your activities is as important as the activity you are engaged in. Too often you are distracted, taking attention away from the activity you are engaged in. "When you are in the *flow* of an activity you are *fully engaged* in the activity for its own sake, not for external rewards. The activity in and of itself brings you a rewarding experience" (19, p. 79). Participating in sports and physical activity can enhance the quality of physical and mental health. Leisure activities can increase friendships and skill development, promote physical well-being, and also may help express parts of your identity. A study that reviewed literature from 1990–2004 on children's and adults' reasons for participation and non-participation in sports and physical activity revealed that weight management, social interaction, and enjoyment were common reasons for participating in sports and physical activity. Concerns about maintaining a slim body shape motivated participation among young girls, and older people identified the importance of sport and physical activity in putting off the effects of aging while providing a social support network (20, p. 826). Physical activity was found to help in coping with diabetes-related stressors in Aboriginal subjects with diabetes (21, p. 321). Your body is engineered to move, and when you deprive your body of activity you begin to experience muscle aches, atrophy, and obesity. It almost as if you are going against nature by living a sedentary life.

A study of 65 nurses regarding three leisure activities found that leisure satisfaction was not related to demographic factors, but to the type of activity (22, p.50). One size does not fit all when reviewing women and leisure (23). A study of women and exercise revealed that some women felt calm when exercising alone and others found the experience most enjoyable if outdoors. A person's perception of time has been found to influence the choice of leisure activities rather than the activity itself (24, p. 405). Research has found that personality, affect, and motivation determined a person's involvement in leisure activity rather than gender, ethnicity, or race (25, p. 470). These findings point to the fact that how one perceives the exercise experience can account for the psychological benefits (26, p. 88). When you choose your activities it is best to find activities that you enjoy, which will most likely increase your willingness to participate. Most important, you need to be active, and give yourselves permission to have playtime everyday.

"Time spent laughing is time spent with the gods" (27, p. 176). Think of the feelings you have after a good laugh. Your entire body responds and tingles in a good way. We cannot forget the importance of laughter when adding rest, relaxation, and recreation into our lives. Laughter has both short-term and long-term benefits:

> *In the short term, a bout of laughter appears to initiate the stress response, with a slight increase in heart rate, blood pressure, muscle tension and ventilations. But this is quickly followed by a rebound effect, where these parameters decrease to below previous resting levels. The over all affect is a profound level of homeostasis and an immune system boost. Laughter is also credited with stabilizing blood pressure, 'massaging' vital organs, stimulating circulation, facilitating digestion and increasing oxygenated blood throughout the body. (28, p. 271)*

When children play you usually hear laughter. Norman Cousins cured himself of a terminal illness by making sure he spent many hours a day laughing. As far as we know, there are no negative side effects to laughter, or added calories, so why not increase and indulge! Let's explore some ways to enjoy more rest, relaxation, and recreation in your life.

### *Life Design Checklist for Rest, Relaxation, and Recreation*

How often do you get eight to nine hours of sleep per night? If you are not getting enough sleep, what is your experience?

_______________

_______________

_______________

What are the ways in which you experience relaxation? If you are not getting enough, what prevents you from relaxing?

_______________

_______________

_______________

What do you do for recreation?

_______________

_______________

_______________

Do you feel that you laugh enough? If you do, describe your experience. If not, what gets in the way?

_______________

_______________

_______________

### My Three Strategies

What I am willing to do today to be successful in adding more rest, relaxation, and recreation to my life:

1. _______________

   _______________

2. _______________

   _______________

3. _______________

   _______________

## Designer Activities

*(These **activities** will help you achieve your **strategies**.)*

*Mindful Meditation*

- Find a space where you will not be interrupted.
- Find a sitting position that is comfortable.
- Pay attention to your breath.
- Scan your body; with each breath release any tension that you are aware of.
- Continue focusing on the breath.
- Very gently rock back and forth. Pay attention only to the rocking.
- If you are interrupted by thoughts, acknowledge them and let them go without judgment.
- What are you aware of?

*Mindful Sensory Awareness*

- Pay attention to your breath.
- Imagine a place in your mind that is peaceful and nurturing.
- Allow yourself to explore.
- Notice the experience of your senses: sight, sound, smell, taste, body and environment temperature.
- Notice the feelings that arise.
- Continue to pay attention to the breath.

*Blissful Back Stretch*

- Lie down on your belly.
- Take a few breaths.
- Place your hands on the floor a few inches above your shoulders.
- Press your pelvis gently into the floor.
- Without pressing into your hands, lift your chest with the energy of your breath. Do this a few times.
- Now press your hands into the floor and lift your chest (you will notice a slight squeeze in the buttocks, which will protect your lower back).
- Come up to your full extension, your edge.
- Breathe.
- Then come down slowly, breathing all the way down.
- Rest and relax.

*Relax and Let Go*

- Move onto your back.
- Allow your body to come into a comfortable position; use a pillow or blanket if needed.
- Bring your arms out to a "T."
- Let your legs and feet relax.

- Put your mind into your shoulders and hands.
- Imagine and experience them becoming heavy, relaxed, and warm.
- Close your eyes.
- Pay attention to your breath.
- Rest and relax.

*Aromatherapy*

- Run a warm bath.
- Combine tangerine, lavender, and geranium oil.
- Play your favorite soothing music.
- Notice your breath.
- Soak for 30 to 45 minutes.
- Enjoy the scents.
- Think positive thoughts.

*Play*

- Find a friend, partner or child to join you in a game (board game, sport, etc.).
- Allow yourself to immerse yourself in the experience with no expectations.

Notice the experience of your thoughts, body, and emotions.

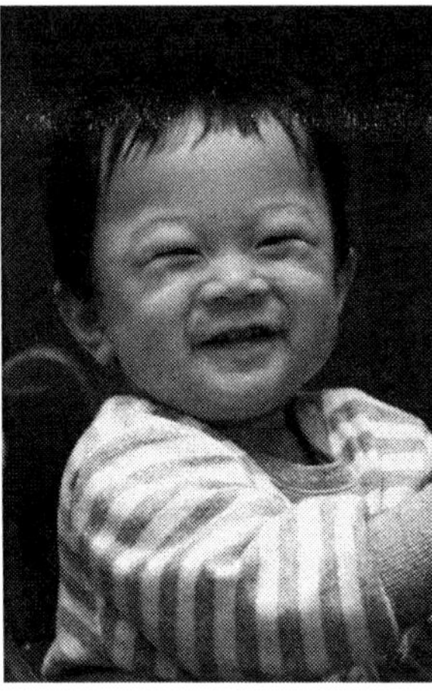



*Laughter*

Watch your favorite comedy movie or show and observe how you feel when you laugh.

Body______________________________________________

Attitude____________________________________________

Mind______________________________________________

## Reference


(1) Cotte, J. (2002). Timestyle and leisure decisions. *Journal of Leisure Research, 33*(4), 396–409.

(2) Davis, J. (2004, July). Psychological benefits of nature experiences: An outline of research and theory. *Naropa University and School of Lost Borders,* 1–9.

(3) deGroot, Redford, G. (2008, March/April). Your brain on exercise. *Arizona Association of Retired People Magazine.* Retrieved from http://www.health.harvard.edu

(4) Schoenborn, C. A., & Barnes, P. M. (2002, April 7). Leisure-time physical activity among adults: United States, 1997–98. *Advance Data from Vital and Health Statistics*, no. 325. Retrieved January 24, 2004, from http://www.cdc.gov/nchs/data/ad/ad325.pdf

(5) Levey, J., & Levey, M. (1998). *Living in balance: A dynamic approach for creating harmony and wholeness in a chaotic world.* Berkeley, CA: Conari Press.

(6) Carr, E. R. (2007). Quality of life for our patients: How media images and messages influence their perceptions. *Clinical Journal of Oncology Nursing, 12*, 43–51.

(7) Gordan-Larsen, P., McMurray, R., & Popkin, B. (2000). Determinants of adolescent physical activity and inactivity patterns. *Pediatrics, 105*(6), 424–430.

(8) Sarang, P., & Telles, S. (2006). Effects of two yoga based relaxation techniques on heart rate variability (HRV). *International Journal of Stress Management, 13*(4), 460–475.

(9) Solomons, S. (2005). Using aromatherapy massage to increase shared attention behaviors in children with autistic spectrum disorders and severe learning difficulties. *British Journal of Special Education, 32*(3), 127–137.

(10) Harvard Health Publications. (2206). The importance of sleep and health. Harvard Women's Health Watch Press Release.

(11) eMedicine, Health Emergency Care and Consumer Health. (2007). Sleep: Understanding the basics. Retrieved from http://www.emedicinehealth.com/script/main/art.asp?articlekey=59

(12) Frank, M. A., & Gustafson, S. (2001). The reciprocal influence of self-esteem and exercise. Retrieved January 24, 2004, from http://www.behavioralconsultants.com/exercise_&_self-esteem.htm

(13) Pohl, S. L., Borrie, W. T., & Patterson, M. E. (2000). Woman, wilderness, and everyday life: A documentation of the connection between wilderness recreation and women's everyday lives. *Journal of Leisure Research*, *32*(4), 415–434.

(14) Ho, C.-H., Payne, L., & Orsega, E. (2003, April). *Parks, recreation and public health*. Retrieved October 21, 2003, from http://www.nrpa.org/story.cfm? story_id=1586&departmentID=18

(15) American Recreation Coalition (ARC). (2000). *Outdoor recreation in America 2000: Addressing key societal concerns.* Washington, DC: Roper Starch. Retrieved January 22, 2002, from http://www.funoutdoors.com/Rec00/

(16) Ericson, N. (2001, May). The YMCA's Teen Action Agenda. *Office of Juvenile Justice and Delinquency Prevention Fact Sheet*, no.14. Retrieved January 24, 2004, from http://www.ncjrs.org/pdffiles1/ojjdp/ fs200114.pdf

(17) Estes, C., & Henderson, K. (2003). Enjoyment and the good life. *Parks and Recreation Magazine, 38*(2), 22–31.

(18) Pagano, I. S., Barkhoff, H., & Heiby, E. M. (2006). Dynamical modeling of the relations between leisure activities and health indicators. *Journal of Leisure Research, 38*, 61–77.

(19) Lama, D., & Cutler, H.C. (2003). The art of happiness at work. New York: Riverhead Books.

(20) Allender, Cowburn, & Foster. (2006, July). Understanding participation in sport and physical activity among children and adults: a review of qualitative studies *Health Education research: Theory and Practice, 2*(6), 826–835.

(21) Iwasaki, Y., & Bartlett, J. (2006). Culturally meaningful leisure as a way of coping with stress among Aboriginal individuals with diabetes. *Journal of Leisure Research, 38*(3), 321–338.

(22) DiBona, L. (2000, February). What are the benefits of leisure? An exploration using the leisure satisfaction. *The British Journal of Occupational Therapy*, *63*(2), 50–58.

(23) Henderson, K. A., Hodges, S., & Kivel, B. (2002, June 1). Context and dialogue in research on women and leisure. *Journal of Leisure Research.*

(24) Cotte, J. (2001). Timestyle and Leisure decision. *Journal of Leisure Research, 33*(4), 396–409. Barnett, L. A. (2006). Accounting for leisure preferences from within: The relative contributors of gender, race or ethnicity, personality, affective style and motivational orientation. *Journal of Leisure Research, 38*(4), 445–474.

(25) Barnett, L.A. (2006) Accounting for leisure preferences from within: the relative contributors of gender, race or ethnicity, personality, affective style and motivational orientation. *Journal of Leisure Research,* 38(4), 445–474.

(26) Plante, T. G., Gores, C., Brecht, C., Carrow, J., Imbs, A., & Willemsen, E. (2007). Does exercise environment enhance the psychological benefits of exercise for women? *International Journal of Stress Management, 14*(1), 88–98.

(27) Dyer, W. W. (1998). *Wisdom of the ages: A modern master brings eternal truths into everyday life.* New York: Harper Collins.

(28) Seaward, B. L. (2006). *Managing stress: Principles and strategies for health and well-being.* Sudbury, MA: Jones and Bartlett Publishers.

# CHAPTER 6

© Jouke van Keulen, 2011. Used under license from Shutterstock, Inc.

# Building Rewarding Relationships

*Open your heart everywhere you go. Send love to everyone you encounter then send it back to yourself.*

Feeling the touch of a gentle hand, sharing a warm embrace, experiencing unconditional love, and knowing there is someone to share dreams and sorrows all create the bond of a human relationship, and hopefully one that is rewarding. Relationships are the food that nourishes our emotional, physical, and spiritual selves. Much of your daily thoughts, activities, and conversations is focused on the relationships you have or wish you had. With all the energy and desire we give to relationships, why is it that so many of us are unhappy in our relationships? We yearn to be connected, yet maintaining harmonious relationships is often a challenge. The need to be connected to significant others begins at birth and is the first ingredient to forming a healthy emotional attachment. "People with a strong support network live longer, are less vulnerable to getting sick, and tend to live happier, more fulfilling lives and children who have strong, supportive relationships with their families were less prone to getting sick, and less likely to turn to drugs, get pregnant, or be involved in crime" (1). Let's take a look at how your early experiences set the stage for developing your personality and how you form relationships.

© Danilo Sanino, 2011. Used under license from Shutterstock, Inc.

### *Primary and Disowned Self*

Hal and Sidra Stone's concept of the *primary and disowned self* is a simple model that describes how we develop the patterns of emotions, thoughts, and behaviors that define us. We develop our primary selves during our growing years when we identify ourselves with *experiences and values* that were accepted by our families and caregivers. These patterns of thinking, feeling, and behaving are the cornerstone of the *primary self,* the person you are familiar with and show to the world. On the other hand, the parts of you that were *rejected* in the growing-up process are the parts of yourself that have not been nurtured, yet are still very much an important part of who you are. This *disowned self*, like the primary self, maintains an equal amount of power in your life. There may be many disowned selves waiting to be acknowledged. Both your primary and disowned selves make up your personality and dictate how you behave in your relationships.

For example, if you were raised in a family where holding your feelings inside was accepted and speaking your mind was frowned upon, you probably will seek out relationships with others who have a voice and speak up for themselves. Unfortunately, your primary self may go along with decisions that you may not agree with. This sets the relationship up for never-ending expectations for someone else to satisfy your disowned self. Letting go of the fear of speaking up for yourself will offer you an opportunity to feel empowered and let go of the expectation of your partner to speak up for you and have the last say. Thus, letting go of your disowned self releases you from being stuck in the "negative dance" of expectations that never seems to end. You repeat old patterns with your children, friends, and family for generations when your disowned selves are hidden, and thus happiness eludes you.

Remember your primary self is that part of yourself that you feel most comfortable with, for better or worse. The disowned self is that part of you that did not receive acceptance, and you, unfortunately, look for that part of yourself in your partners, children, employers, coworkers, and friends, seeking to have these needs of the disowned self met. You search out others to satisfy those parts of yourself that you have disowned and rejected by expecting others to meet those needs (2). In fact, you often choose partners who mirror those parts of yourself that you reject. Take a moment and reflect upon the characteristics that define your *primary self* and those characteristics that define your *disowned self* and how these show up in your relationships.

*All you need is love, love, love*

Infants thrive on being soothed when in pain, want to be held for safety and comfort, and seek out consistent nurturing from the familiarity of caregivers. Infants form attachment by the love they receive from their caregivers in rocking, hugs, coos, and smiles taken in through their senses. These experiences are transformed by the infant's sensory systems into patterned neuronal activity that influences the development of the brain in positive ways, helping infants to grow and survive (3). When babies feel nurtured in their relationships, they readily learn to become interdependent with others. For example, a baby may reach out to a parent and give the parent his or her toy or offer to share his or her food. Infants readily offer smiles and hugs and soothe a distressed parent by stroking the parent's face or offering a kiss. This is the beginning of developing empathy, a core ingredient in healthy relationships. Even at this early stage of growing, infants are forming the primary self, learning how to receive love and acceptance.

The relationship between a parent and child can be one of the most transforming experiences in your life, as children are mirrors of you. If you pay attention to what's happening with your children,

© Dawn Hudson, 2011. Used under license from Shutterstock, Inc.

you see the deepest part of yourself, like it or not! "It's interesting to look at your children as live-in Zen masters who can put their finger on places where you're resistant, or thinking narrowly, in ways no one else can", (4). Children help you seek out the "child within yourself." It is not unusual to find a big, burly dad rolling on the floor, laughing heartily with his toddler, only to go back into a silent shell when connecting with his partner or friends. Your life can be richer if you sustain that magic and sense of vulnerability with all of your experiences. When you allow your vulnerability to be seen, you open the doors for intimacy and empathy in your relationships, the road to happiness. Imagine how fulfilling life could be!

© Dawn Hudson, 2011. Used under license from Shutterstock, Inc.

Relationships during adolescence are a crucial time and a stepping-stone toward adulthood. Too often parents worry about the negative impact of romantic relationships with adolescents, such as risky sexual activity and abusive behaviors. When adolescents engage in healthy romantic relationships it can have a positive impact on (a) identity, which can help them gain a clearer understanding of who they are and what they value; (b) developing interpersonal skills through effective communication, negotiating boundaries, developing empathy and emotional resiliency, and coping skills during break-ups; and (c) receiving emotional support from those other than parents (5), particularly for minority sexual orientation youth who often keep their sexual orientation a secret from family and friends, as their romantic partner may be the only person they feel safe sharing thoughts and feelings with (6). Helping adolescents process feelings and express the nuances of their experiences in their relationships with their friends and adults without the fear of judgment can support them in making healthy decisions. When parents, friends, and teachers accept the ups and downs of adolescent relationships with respect by responding to them without reacting or judgment, they are able to model empathy. Acknowledging adolescents with all of their drama, emotions, and behaviors leads them on the road toward open, healthy relationships as they mature into adulthood.

© docent, 2011. Used under license from Shutterstock, Inc.

College-age students, like adolescents, often have ideals pertaining to relationships. Research studying undergraduate students found that 62% of those students involved in a relationship believed that "all problems can be solved if there is enough love," and men as well as women believed in "love at first sight" and "love conquers all" (7). A study that looked at college students' beliefs about romantic relationships found that men were more likely to believe that living together improved marriage, bars were a good place to meet a mate, men control relationships, and people will "cheat" if they feel they will not get caught. Women, on the other hand, were more likely to believe that love is more important than factors such as age and race in choosing a mate, that couples stop "trying" after they marry, and that women know when their men are lying (8). Students in university settings often seek help related to love relationships that are interfering with their academic success and retention. Some college-age students may for the first time live away from the guidance of their families. They are left to navigate their way in the world of relationships—making new friends, having the freedom to engage in sexual activity, figuring out ways to manage time for academic study and employment, and having the pressure of knowing that they hold their future in their hands.

All too often, young adults enter the world ill equipped emotionally to handle the plethora of experiences and decisions they need to make. If young adults are lacking the emotional ammunition to engage successfully, we can help them along the way. Offering courses for students beginning in elementary school through college that focus on healthy relationships may be as important as the academic curriculum so that they gain life skills in developing harmony and happiness. After all, the wisdom one develops from life experiences, usually as a result of relationship experiences, is the impetus to use the knowledge gained.

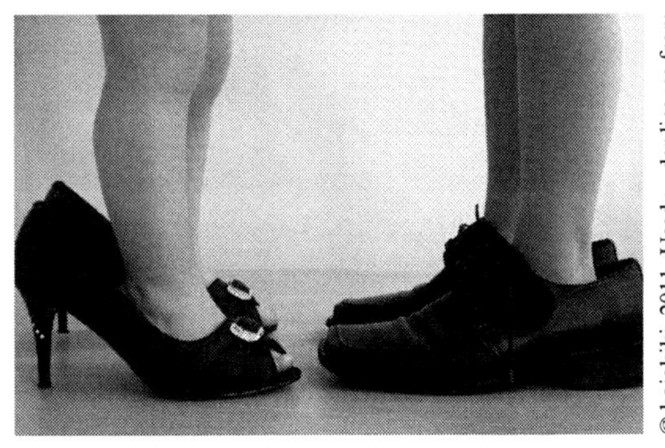



As adults we continue to long for connection. "Relationships are living organisms that, like plants and animals, need nutrients to survive. Neglect lead to starvation, atrophy, root rot and eventual death of the human spirit" (9, p. 171). We need each other, yet often excessive demands are placed on relationships, sucking the joy out of them. Parents want to dictate a child's life, friends make unrealistic demands, and partners fear rejection and lose the wonder of intimacy in their relationship. Regardless of whom you are in relationships with, there is one steadfast common factor: you are the main character in all of your relationships. We all want to be happy, yet often cannot find the tools to achieve harmony.

We often load our relationships with expectations, demands, misperceptions, fear of intimacy, and projections. These frequently lead to conflict and anxiety and thus disconnection, the very opposite of our desire. A sense of self-satisfaction impacts our feelings in our relationships with others. This is a key element in sustaining a rewarding relationship. Reflecting back on the previous discussion of development of the self, it becomes clear that adults who cannot accept their own experiences without judgment will undoubtedly place unrealistic demands on their relationships with others. These expectations propel a vicious cycle of demanding and longing to receive from others that which we need to give ourselves. How can you unravel the patterns of behaviors you have developed that prevent you from having rewarding relationships? Researchers continue to ask couples what works to maintain satisfaction together, offering you guidance in your own relationships.

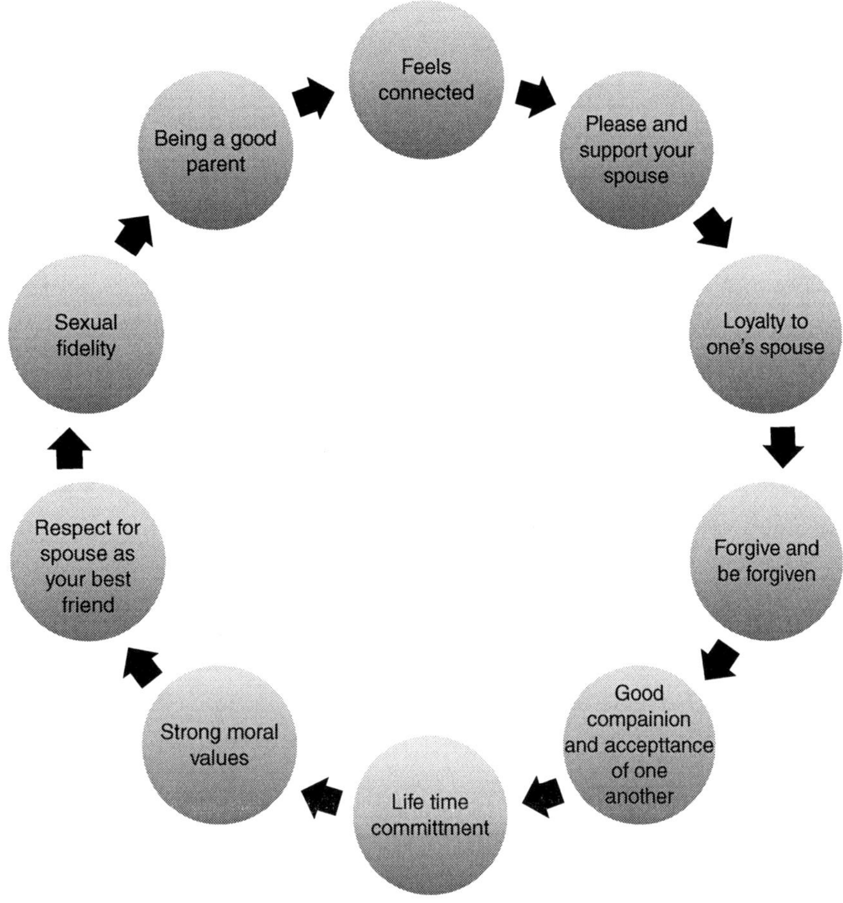


Ten most important characteristics of couples married over twenty years (10, p. 160)

| Six Behaviors Important to Relationship Satisfaction | | | | | |
|---|---|---|---|---|---|
| Acknowledging the partner | Engaging the partner in everyday conversations | Ego- building comments such as praising | Share memories about time together | Share mutual activities | Give feedback, mutual honesty, encouragement and correction |

*Source: (11, p. 311)*

A feeling of being connected and acceptance of the other are themes found in rewarding relationships. Couples who are mentally engaged, open to new experiences, and aware of new contexts enjoy more satisfying and fulfilling marital relationships. Mindful individuals may feel less threatened by change (12, p. 50). Sometimes people need guidance to see relationships from a new perspective, as many of us are fixed in particular ways of behaving, feeling, and thinking, repeating the same patterns in relationships for generations. How often does one say, "I can't believe I'm doing the same thing as my mother, or father!" The Relationship Enhancement System is one model to help us navigate away from old behaviors and toward developing new healthy relationships.

| Relationships Enhancement System | |
|---|---|
| Expressive (Owning Skill) | One is aware of and owns his or her feelings |
| Empathic Responding (Receptive Skill) | One listens and gains an understanding of the other person's feelings and motives |
| Conversive (Discussion/Negotiation/ Engagement Skill) | One learns to listen and give back a sense of understanding of the meaning of what was heard |

*Source: (13, p. 309)*

Even if you have developed skills for maintaining a healthy relationship, you need to be able to handle the challenges that face you so that you can regain balance and harmony. Guttmann found that marital success depended upon maintaining a ratio of five positive experiences to one negative, regardless of whether the marital conflict style was marked by validation, volatility, or avoidance (14, p. 265). When partners in a marriage are optimistic, they understand that conflicts are natural, can be confined to many of successive situations, are always resolvable, and that each partner has the skills to fulfill these expectations (15, p. 264). The following questions reflect optimism, thus facilitating a more positive marital interaction and outcome. Note that these questions are not dictating opinions and "shoulds," but rather, an openness for both to process and share:

*How soon can we get back to feeling good with each other?*
*What are my resources to resolve this most successfully?*
*What are the best questions to get us on a good track?*
*Is this an optimum time to discuss this?*
*What can we learn so we do better next time?*
*What solutions would have us both win? (16)*

Take a moment and reflect upon your *friendships.* Do you feel nourished or depleted in your friendships? We often reflect upon the significant impact a friend has had or has in our lives. Friendships are one of the first relationships we develop away from our family that offer us new opportunities to explore ourselves, often without expectations. A longitudinal study of 32 years found that people were 57% more likely to become obese if a friend became obese. The impact of family had less influence than friends, regardless of whether they lived 100 miles away or 15 (17). Research has also found that when women are stressed they elicit the hormone oxytocin, which is calming and buffers the fight-or-flight response, encouraging them to reach out to other women. Women also tend to seek the company of other women

© AirOne, 2011. Used under license from Shutterstock, Inc.

when stressed (18). It is a known fact that women live longer than men, and this may be due to the fact that women are one of the best buffers toward preventing illness. Men have a different way of dealing with their relationships with their friends—their "conversations deal with the doing of things rather than the feelings of things." Research has found that men do not choose friends or partners who are demanding or needy, and men are not usually physically or emotionally expressive, yet derive great support from their friendships (19) Regardless of how men and women interact and gain support from each other, the fact remains that friendships are often the backbone of emotional satisfaction for both.

For older adults, the need for love and connection does not dwindle. Unfortunately, in our Western world the media depicts older adults as frail and ill. The fact is older adults have wisdom to share, like to play, enjoy engaging in conversation with others, and desire intimacy. Changing the attitudes of young and middle-aged adults toward the elderly is necessary so that the expression of sexuality and desire for intimacy is viewed as important. As a society we hold cultural beliefs that restrict the most basic needs of older adults, and "this cultural ambivalence, then, seems to be interfering with the physical, psychological and material well-being of older adults" (20). Research has found that elderly persons who enjoy an active sex life and intimate relationships report more life satisfaction than those who do not. The need to be touched, stroked, cuddled, and caressed is lifelong. Physical contact is as significant in persons age 70 and 80 as in infancy (21, p. 226–227). Human beings, regardless of age, have the same basic needs. When we remove the judgment of how we perceive elders, children and adolescents will move toward a more harmonious society as they age.

Emotional security and companionship have been found to be core elements to happiness in relationships (22, p. 257). Surprisingly, research has found that income has little to do with achieving happiness in relationships (23). Research has found that "people with stronger materialistic values reported more negative emotions and less relatedness, autonomy, competence, gratitude, and meaning in life" (24, p. 521). When people are grateful they spend less time striving for things materialistic and more time leading a meaningful life and cultivating quality relationships, (25, p. 356). You may often find yourself in a "rut," engaging in the same activities day after day with no change. This can also affect your level of happiness. Research has found that people with high trait curiosity had more frequent growth-oriented behaviors, and search for meaning and life satisfaction, (26, p. 159). People need to find personal joy, which may positively impact their relationships.

© Elena Ray, 2011. Used under license from Shutterstock, Inc.

When people are happy they are more motivated to engage in kindness toward others (27). It's a win-win relationship when you are happy with yourself because you have a better chance of choosing relationships that are more rewarding. When you are courageous enough to openly self-reflect and share those reflections with another, only then can you truly experience a deep relationship and empathically

© Yaro, 2011. Used under license from Shutterstock, Inc.

step into another's shoes. There are two challenges in maintaining a soulful relationship—knowing yourself and knowing the deep richness in the soul of your partner. When you pay attention to your partner, you find yourself (28, p. 28). Sharing a deep sense of intimacy is the backbone of a healthy relationship.

What is intimacy? Being comfortable with our vulnerability describes intimacy in a nutshell. Intimacy is being in touch with the reality of another person and having a shared internal awareness (29). In order to be comfortable with your vulnerability, you need to let go of fear of rejection, approval seeking, and expectations. "The only way to get acquainted with your snake pit so that you can begin to let go of hating it and learn to embrace and accept it is by –ever so gently and gradually—sharing it with another person" (30, p. 191). Once you can accept yourself you can swim gracefully into self-disclosing to the important people in your life. Self-disclosure is the core of experiencing intimacy. Intimate communication is a dance where both parties are engaged and connecting on various levels—verbal and nonverbal—experiencing each other through sensory stimuli and feeling the exchange of energy.

Taking what we have discussed thus far, how do you sustain the magic in your relationships? Can you accept the unpredictability, autonomy, and mystery in your relationships? Can you accept the uniqueness in each relationship? How wonderful it is that we have the ability to unglue each other from our past and unleash the disowned, unconscious self! Now you have the ingredients to embrace and experience a rewarding relationship with the many possibilities of enchantment and awe.

## Life Design Personal Relationship Checklist

Who are the important people in my life?

______________________________________________

______________________________________________

______________________________________________

What are the expectations I have placed on my relationships?

______________________________________________

______________________________________________

______________________________________________

These are the various characteristics of my disowned self that I am aware of.

______________________________________________

______________________________________________

______________________________________________

I have difficulty listening empathically when…

______________________________________________

______________________________________________

______________________________________________

### My Three Strategies

What I am willing to do today to be successful in creating change in my relationships:

1. ______________________________________________
   ______________________________________________
2. ______________________________________________
   ______________________________________________
3. ______________________________________________
   ______________________________________________

### Life Design Activities

*(These activities will help you achieve your strategies.)*

*1. Empathy toward another*

1. Find a comfortable seated position. Close your eyes. Allow the body to be held by the chair. Notice the bodily sensation of contact with the chair.
2. Relax your abdomen. Notice that the breath is already moving on its own. Follow the breath for a few moments.

3. Bring to mind a visual image or a felt sense of someone who embodied the quality of loving-kindness. Imagine that this person is sitting across from you.
4. Now imagine that you are emanating feelings of gratitude or love toward that person.
5. When your attention wanders, simply return to this image or felt sense of the persona and begin again.

*2. Disowned self—the part of you that is hidden and needs visibility*

1. Make a list of the characteristics that describe you.
2. Make another list of the characteristics that describe the significant people in your life.

Characteristics of self Characteristics of significant others

What are you aware of now?

How are you stuck in old thinking and behavior patterns?

### Mindful Parenting

*Activity 1: Through my child's eyes*

Choose a week for simply noticing your child.
During all of your interactions with your child, see the world from his or her eyes.
Take a moment to reflect on how you would feel being in your child's shoes.
Notice what it feels like to have you as a parent.

*Activity 2: An offering of myself*

Choose a week to simply notice your child.
Every day, spend an hour in an activity with your child.

Listen without interrupting during the entire interaction.
Notice how the interaction is different.
Pay attention to your child.
Pay attention to your body, behavior, thoughts, and interaction.

## Friend Connection

*Activity 1*

Find a quiet place.
Bring the image of a friend into focus.
Think about times spent together.
Create an opportunity to spend time with that friend.

*Activity 2*

Find a quiet place.
Bring the image of a friend into focus.
Make an offering of your heart to your friend.
Share your offering with your friend.

## Exploring my Relationships

Think of the people who share your life. What are the characteristics that make up the relationships? Place the name of someone important to you in the larger center circle and identify the salient characteristics that make up that relationship. (Add more circles if necessary.)

INGREDIENTS OF A REWARDING RELATIONSHIP IN MY LIFE

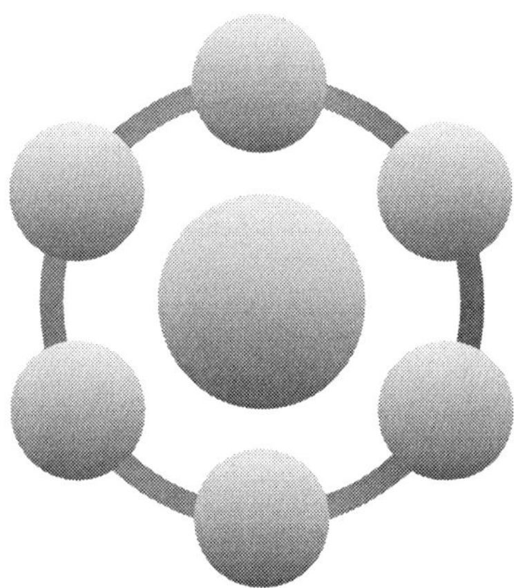

Place the name of that significant person in the larger center circle and reflect on what you would like to say to that person.

WHAT WOULD I LIKE TO SAY TO THAT PERSON THAT EXPRESSES MY LOVE?

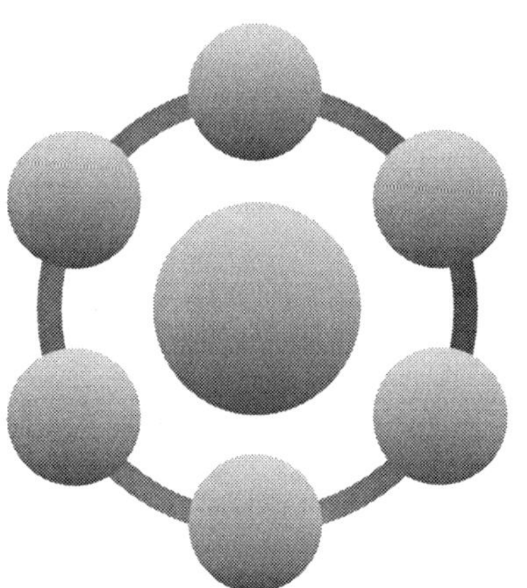

## Reference


(1) Levey, J., & Levey, M. (1998). All my relations. In *Living in balance: A dynamic approach for creating harmony and wholeness in a chaotic world* (p. 200). Berkeley, CA: Conari Press.

(2) Stone, H., & Stone, S. (2007). The psychology of selves in embracing each other. Voice Dialogue International. Retrieved from http://delos-inc.com/Reading_Room/Book_Chapters/EEO/eeo.html

(3) Perry, B. D. (2001, October). Attachment: The first core strength. *Early Childhood Today*.

(4) Kabat-Zinn, J., & Kabat-Zinn, M. (1998). Mindful parenting. *Yes! Magazine.* Spring Millennium Survival Guide.

(5) Sorensen, S. (2007, July). Adolescent romantic relationships. *ACT for Youth Center of Excellence Research Facts and Findings.*

(6) Barber, B., & Eccles, J. (2003). The joy of romance: Healthy adolescent relationships as an educational agenda. In P. Florsheim (Ed.), *Adolescent romantic relationships and sexual behavior: Theory, research and practical implications*. Mahwah, NJ: Lawrence Eribaum Associates.

(7) Know, D., Schacht, C., & Zusman, M. E. (1999, March). Love relationships among college students. *College Student Journal.*

(8) Abowitz, D. A., Knox, D., Zusman, M., & McNeely, A. (2009, June). Beliefs about romantic relationships: Gender differences among undergraduates. *College Student Journal.*

(9) Seaward, B. L. (2004). *Managing stress: Principles and strategies for health and well-being*. Boston: Jones and Bartlett Publishers.

(10) Young, M. A. (2004, April). Healthy relationships: Where's the research? *The Family Journal: Counseling and Therapy for Couples and Families, 12*(2), 159–162.

(11) Schumway, S. T., & Wampler, R. S. (2002). A behaviorally focused measure for relationships: The couple behavior report. *The American Journal of Family Therapy, 30*, 311–321.

(12) Burpee, C., & Langer, E. J. (2005, January). Mindfulness and marital satisfaction. *Journal of Adult Development, 12,* 43–51.

(13) Nichols, M. P., & Schwartz, R. C. (2006). *Family therapy: Concepts and methods*. Boston: Pearson.

(14) Goldberg, M. C. (1998). *The art of the question*. John Wiley & Sons, Inc.

(15) Christakis, N. A., & Fowler, J. H. (2007, July). The spread of obesity in a large social network over 32 years. *The New England Journal of Medicine, 357*, 370–379.

(16) Taylor, S. E., Cousino Klein, L., Lewis, B. P., Gruenewald, T. L., Gurung, R. A. R., & Updegraff, F. A. (2000). Biobehavioral responses to stress in females: Tend-and-befriend, not fight-or-flight. *Psychological Review, 107*(3), 411–429.

(17) Zaslow, J. (2010, April). Friendship for guys (No tears!). *The Wall Street Journal.*

(18) Wood-Aleman, M. (2008, October). Enabling romantic relationships in later life: Discarding cultural myths and facilitation dialogue. *The Oates Journal, 12*(13), 1–8.

(19) Hodson, D. S., & Skeen, P. (1994). Sexuality and aging. *Journal of Applied Gerontology, 13,* 219–234.

(20) Demir, M. (2008). Sweetheart, you really make me happy: romantic relationship quality and personality as predictors of happiness among emerging adults. *Journal of Happiness Studies, 9,* 257–277.

(21) North, R., J, Holahan, C. H., Moos, R. H., & Cronkite, R. C. (2008). Family support, family income and happiness: A 10 year perspective. *Journal of Family Psychology, 22*(3), 475–483.
(22) Kasha, T. B., & Breen, W. E. (2007, May). Materialism and diminished well being: Experiential avoidance as a mediating mechanism. *Journal of Social and Clinical Psychology, 26*(5), 521–539.
(23) Polak, E. L., & Mcullough, M. E. (2006). Is gratitude an alternative to materialism? *Journal of Happiness Studies, 7*, 343–360.
(24) Kashdan, T. B., & Steger, M. F. (2007). Curiosity and pathways to well being and meaning in life: Traits, states, and everyday behaviors. *Motivation and Emotion, 31*, 159–173.
(25) Otake, K., Simai, S., Tanaka-Matsumi, J., Otsui, K., & Fredrickson, B. L. (2006). Happy people become happier through kindness: A counting kindnesses intervention. *Journal of Happiness Studies, 7*, 361–375.
(26) Moore, T. (1994). *Soul mates: Honoring the mysteries of love and relationship*. New York: Harper Perennial.
(27) Mosier, W. (2006, March 22). Intimacy: The key to a healthy relationship. *Annals of the American Psychotherapy Association.*
(28) Page, S. (1994). *Now that I'm married, why isn't everything perfect?* New York: Dell Books.

CHAPTER 7

© Ladyann, 2011. Used under license from Shutterstock, Inc.

# My Passion Discovery

*When work, commitment, and pleasure all become one and you reach that deep well where passion lives, nothing is impossible.*

*~Unknown*

Passion is not something you think about or necessarily feel every day. Yet, when you consider the importance passion plays in your life, you may wonder, why don't you think about it? Is it because you get caught up with just trying to live life? Does passion get beaten down by other people and therefore it is forgotten? Is passion vulnerable to stressors, just like how stressors can stamp out joy? Or, does passion simply not enter your consciousness because it has yet to emerge?

Life without passion is like an ice cream sundae without whipped cream and a cherry on top. All you get is the taste of a cold substance but no delicious sweet joy or Technicolor pleasure.

Why is having passion so important? It is the unification of mind, body, and spirit. It is who you are—your inner desires, feelings, and dreams. It is what drives your core energy and, ultimately, it is what gives you the strength to achieve fulfillment and success.

How can you discover your passion? How can you draw out your inner desires, feelings, and dreams? First, you can simply think about what makes you feel joy or be joyous. Is it the people you live or work with who bring that out in you? Is it the things you do? Is it where you live? Is it the pet you have that you can come home to at the end of the day who loves you only for who you are? Is it the goals or dreams you are currently seeking or those in the back of your mind that you know you need to get to? It may be any of these or other very personal and deep thoughts and emotions.

This is what passion is about. It is fueled by your thoughts and driven by your feelings and emotions. If you think you are able to do something but don't feel you are capable of it, your passion can stall. The reverse is also true. You can feel deeply about something but not have the skill or ability to make it happen. So, awareness of your thoughts/feelings/emotions is the cornerstone to embedding and then engaging passion in your life. Therefore, passion is a state when energy is fully concentrated on a specific and all-important goal that is greater and more important than you are. It is an essential element to any worthwhile achievement (1).

Another consideration in thinking about passion is how and when you feel attraction for yourself, others, and particular experiences. Since you have had unique life experiences you possess special

© Sergey Peterman, 2011. Used under license from Shutterstock, Inc.

desires, likes and dislikes that are unique to you and your life experience. These are important to consider. Do I like myself enough to pursue what is important to me? Am I attracted to others who help me build my life rather than stall it or tear it down? Do I put myself in situations that are healthy and growth producing or do I continually repeat experiences that are challenging, threatening, or self-defeating? Only you can decide if this is your pattern and how you set the "attraction meter" of your life.

Identifying, igniting, and engaging your passion are important and make the difference between a "flatline" life and one that is exciting, excellent, and is seen and felt as fulfilling and successful. The guide below provides the essential ingredients.

**P** = Perspective

**A** = Attitude

**S** = Sensitivity

**S** = Savor

**I** = Interest

**O** = Opportunity

**N** = Nourish

Examine your PERSPECTIVE about what life has been, is now, and what you would like it to be. Look back and then look forward. Use the strategy of meditation or dreaming what you would like to be, to do, to act on or even attempt. Meditation and dreaming are free of charge and can be done whenever and wherever you like. You don't have to reserve it, pay for it, save for it, or ask someone else for it. You can meditate or dream a lot or a little. But, you must first meditate or dream before you can "get in touch" with your passion.

Reflect on your ATTITUDE. The attitude required for being passionate is adopting a positive approach to all that comes your way. Even when the "rain is falling" and you feel there is no end in sight, your attitude can help draw your passion. Passion cannot live and grow in a barren field. It must be nurtured with energy and strength and be an attitude filled with hope and desire.

Check your SENSITIVITY. Be sensitive to yourself and others. This leads you to an understanding as to how you affect others and how they affect you. Your passion can be stalled if you have a "blind eye" to yourself and those around you. The relationships you establish and maintain can be the barriers or, conversely, the promoters of your dreams and passion.

SAVOR each moment in your life. You have 1440 minutes each day. They go quickly and you cannot retrieve the ones that have past. Be in the moment, breathe in—smell, taste, and appreciate every single one of them.

Cultivate your INTEREST. You have to be interested in pursuing what makes you feel passionate to engage in passionate activities. Without interest not much happens. Life becomes stale, bland, and filled with "white noise." Without interest you will not be able to draw enough energy to even think about passion. Become curious. Get interested in everything that comes your way because, who knows, one of those interesting things that does come your way might just be the passion you were looking for.

Seek **OPPORTUNITY.** Every day there are multitudes of opportunities. The trick is being aware of them and then knowing they are staring you in the face. These opportunities are the avenues for you to ignite and engage in your passion. For example, say your passion is to write a book just like this one. You happen to mention this desire to a friend. The mentioning of the book becomes the opportunity because this friend has a colleague who publishes these types of books and can arrange an introduction. The opportunity led you down a tangible path to igniting and then engaging in your passion, writing the book. Simple!

**NOURISH** your passion. Make sure you focus on, think and dream about, and then act on your passion each and every day. It is only through your continued energy that it will stay lit. Give passion your attention and your intention.

Vallerand (2) has been researching passion for several years. He provides a new conceptualization of passion called the Dualistic Model of Passion. In his model he aligns passion with activities and asserts that passion is a strong inclination to an activity that an individual likes, finds important, and is willing to invest time and energy in. The dualistic nature of passion is expressed in his codification of passion as harmonious passion and obsessive passion. Harmonious passion is the internalization of passion as an activity in which an individual has "free will" in determining engagement. That is, the passion for the activity is not overpowering but rather integrated into the individual's life space. Conversely, obsessive passion is defined as leading the individual to having an uncontrollable urge to engage in the activity. There is no "free will" but rather the passion itself drives the person to possible conflict and discomfort as decisions are made based on the passion as the "driver." This model provides an interesting premise regarding the power of passion; it can either enhance or interfere with the quality of your life.

In their research, Duckworth, Peterson, Matthews, and Kelly (3) found that "grit" (passion and perseverance for long-term goals) can predict positive outcomes. Passion has its own energy; observable and transferable. It will enable you to overcome obstacles and see infinite potential (4).

Passion also brings joy, and joy is what makes life "worth living"—passion is a vital element of happiness. Joy is what connects you to your deepest feelings and engages others to want to be a part of what you are about. Joy is simply an ingredient of life that we often forget to think about. So, joy leads to happiness and happiness is joyful. Sounds cyclic and it is... just the endless cycle you want to be in.

How do you achieve happiness? Well this can only happen if you want it to. Being emotionally happy means you see the world as a place in which you can find joy and be engaged in all the activities that appear "in front of you." Remember that this is not an unconscious process. It is desired consciousness—being mindful of what is happening "in that moment." Does this mean everything is always wonderful? Not at all. It means that you find meaning in each aspect of your life.

The scientific study of what makes life worth living is *positive psychology*. It underscores that what is good in life is as important as what may be bad (5). Seligman and Csikszentmihalyi (6) assert that positive psychology is about "valued subjective experiences." This includes well-being, contentment, satisfaction (with the past), hope and optimism (for the future), and flow and happiness (in the present). For individuals it is about positive individual traits. Seligman, Parks, and Steen (7) concluded that there are three constituents of happiness: pleasure (positive emotion or being happy), engagement (gratification), and life meaning (a purpose in life).

What is most significant about being happy is that research has found that happiness leads to desirable outcomes at school and at work and even to good health. And, happiness can be taught (5). Studies have revealed a "set point" for happiness, similar to a set point for weight. Therefore, some people who have a high set point do not have to work as hard—they are just happy! Further research on set points found that only 50% of happiness is determined by the set point itself, with 10% attributed to life circumstance. This leaves 40% of the capacity for happiness within the power of an individual to change (8).

There is an adage that happiness is not having what you want, but wanting what you have. Larsen and McKibban (9) indeed found that wanting what you have and having what you want accounts for happiness.

Recent Gallup-Healthways Well-Being Index results (10) from a random survey of more 29,000 Americans, ages 18 and older, living in all 50 states, revealed that the respondents rated their lives better at the start of the year than in any other month since tracking was initiated in 2008. For example, the "thriving" percentage went up to 54.2% from 49% in 2008. Fewer respondents perceived themselves as "struggling" (42.6%) compared with 47% three years earlier. These higher thriving scores came from the perception that the 41% of Americans surveyed stated that they felt the economy was getting better. The premise of the survey is to represent how Americans rate themselves with regard to what they consider the worst to the best possible life. Those who saw themselves as thriving had met their basic needs, had higher incomes, and were less burdened by illness. They had what they wanted and wanted what they had. Moreover, they reported on their happiness through a description of what they considered positive days. Five Americans reported positive days for every individual who reported a negative day (11). Further, a study by Dunn, Aknin, and Norton (12) found that when people were asked to spend money on others they experienced greater happiness.

Being happy is also thinking and talking happy. Thinking happy is being mindful. Being in the present allows you to be curious about your feelings. When negative emotions occur they lose their impact because you are able to engage rather than react! Talking happy is finding ways to positively communicate with yourself and others. This means that sarcasm, cynicism, negative self-talk, as well as being "mean spirited" are forms of communication that need to be put in your past. These communication patterns are not ones that are engaging nor are they singularly clear. For example, being sarcastic is a form of communication that offers a double message to the other person. The other person is never sure if you are serious about what you are talking about and therefore the message itself is lost and the other person is left only with a feeling of potential anger, frustration, or perhaps feeling insignificant or hurt. So being able to "spin" messages to the upside and bringing forward your happiness and joy is clearly a way to endlessly being happy. It is up to you!

Having passion is a necessity for a fulfilling and successful life. It is a free commodity. Make haste. It is there waiting for you. You just have to look within and there it will be!

## Life by Design Passion Checklist

Reflect on the following questions to determine the extent to which you are currently blending passion into your life space and activities.

What do you do, feel, think about, and/or act on that excites you?

______________________________________________

______________________________________________

______________________________________________

What activities make you feel fulfilled and productive?

______________________________________________

______________________________________________

______________________________________________

Whom do you feel most passionate about? Why? How do these same people make you feel?

______________________________________________

______________________________________________

______________________________________________

Do you dream? If so, what do you typically dream about? What meaning do those dreams have?

______________________________________________

______________________________________________

______________________________________________

List the desires you have for your future. Describe how you might realize those.

______________________________________________

______________________________________________

______________________________________________

Think about the last time you felt joy and were completely happy. Describe the situation that made you feel completely happy.

______________________________________________

______________________________________________

______________________________________________

### My Three Strategies

What I am willing to do today to discover and engage my passion:

1. ______________________________________________
______________________________________________
2. ______________________________________________
______________________________________________
3. ______________________________________________
______________________________________________

### Designer Activities

*(These activities will help you achieve your strategies.)*

- Describe what drives you to do positive things for yourself and others. List these and determine how often in a week you do these.
- What was the last dream you had, whether awake or asleep? What was its significance to you?
- What dreams do you have that help you set your life goals?
- Without any artificial barriers, what are your greatest joys? Do you experience these daily and, if not, why? What would help you integrate these joys into your daily life?
- Draw a picture of you completely happy.

# My Passion Discovery
## REFLECTIVE JOURNAL

*Here is your opportunity to write down your "real" intention for becoming aware, igniting and engaging in your passion. Use this Passion Reflective Journal to describe the ways you will explore, find, and then live out your passion. Don't forget to list any barriers you may encounter and how you will overcome them.*

______________________________________________________________________

______________________________________________________________________

______________________________________________________________________

______________________________________________________________________

______________________________________________________________________

______________________________________________________________________

______________________________________________________________________

______________________________________________________________________

______________________________________________________________________

______________________________________________________________________

## Reference

(1) Comeau, R. (2010, December 21). Don't cheat yourself: Live with passion. Retrieved from http://www.articlesbase.com
(2) Vallerand, R. J. (2008). On the psychology of passion: In search of what makes people's lives most worth living. *Canadian Psychology, 49*(1), 1–13.
(3) Duckworth, A. L., Peterson, C., Matthews, M. D., & Kelly, D. R. (2007). Grit: Perseverance and passion for long-term goals. *Journal of Personality and Social Psychology, 92*(6), 1087–1101.
(4) Norris, B. (2010). What is passion? Retrieved from http://briannorris.com
(5) Peterson, C. (2008, May 16). The good life. Positive psychology, and what makes life worth living? *Psychology Today.* Retrieved from http://www.psychologytoday.com/
(6) Seligman, M. E. P., & Csikszentmihalyi, M. (2000). Positive psychology. *American Psychologist, 55*(1), 5–14.
(7) Seligman, M. E. P., Parks, A. C., & Steen, T. (2004). A balanced psychology and a full life. *Philosophical Transactions of the Royal Society, 359,* 1379–1381.
(8) Lyubomirsky, S. (2008). *The how of happiness: A scientific approach to getting the life you want.* New York: Penguin Press.
(9) Larsen, J. T., & McKibban, A. R. (2008). Is happiness having what you want, wanting what you have, or both? *Psychological Science, 19*(4), 371–377.
(10) Mendes, E. (2011). Americans' life evaluation climbs to three-year high. Gallup Poll. Retrieved from http://www.gallup.com/poll/
(11) Arora, R., & Harter, J. (2008). Nearly as many Americans struggling as thriving. Gallup Poll. Retrieved from http://www.gallup.com/poll/
(12) Dunn, E. W., Aknin, L. B., & Norton, M. I. (2008). Spending money on others promotes happiness. *Science, 39*, 1687–1688.

## Other Readings to Explore

Cassidy, G. (2000). *Discovering your passion: An intuitive search to find your purpose in life.* Westfield, NJ: Tomlyn Publishers.
Diener, D. (2008). *Happiness: Unlocking the mysteries of psychological wealth.* Hoboken, NJ: Wiley-Blackwell.
Gilbert, D. (2005). *Stumbling on happiness.* New York: Vintage Books.
Holahan, C. K., Holahan, C. J., Velazquez, K. E., & North, R. J. (2008). Longitudinal change in happiness during aging: The predictive role of positive expectancies. *International Journal of Aging and Human Development, 66*(3), 229–241.
How to buy happiness. (2007). *Futurist, 41*(5), 6.
Layard, R. (2005). *Happiness: Lessons from a new science.* Westminster, London: Penguin Press.
Richardson, H. (1994). Proceed with passion. *Transportation & Distribution, 35*(4), 68.
Self fulfilling prophecies. (2007, August). *University at Berkeley Wellness Letter, 23*(11), 8.
Seligman, M. (2011). *Flourish: A visionary new understanding of happiness and well-being.* New York: Free Press.
Seligman, M. E. P. (2004). *Authentic happiness: Using the new positive psychology to realize your potential for lasting fulfillment.* New York: Free Press/Simon and Schuster.

# CHAPTER 8

# Personal Visioning

*The future belongs to those who believe in the beauty of their dreams.*

*~Eleanor Roosevelt*

Personal visioning is not typically something you stop and do or include in your daily activities, yet it has great influence on how you conduct your life. Does your life seem controlled by other forces/people, or do you feel like you are in a center of a cyclone, or perhaps you find yourself sitting on the outside of the world looking in? If any of these situations are occurring, then it is time to for you to stop and set forth your personal vision. Sounds easy, right? Well not really. It will take some time and your intention.

Personal visioning requires insight into all aspects of your life. Much of what we have discussed in *Life by Personal Design* has offered opportunities for you to become more aware of your own unique self and ways you can perceive and manage your life. Why is personal visioning so important? Without a vision you never have a full understanding of you, as an individual, and the manner in which you want to conduct your life. Personal visioning allows you to link your current and future life events and actions with your values and priorities, helps you make the kind of choices that can lead to work-life balance, and it offers you the ability to set goals and a personal action plan that will incorporate your passion and your self-intentioned changes.

Although you may not be aware of it, visioning has been a part of your developmental growth. What your vision was as a young child, teenager, young adult, at midlife, and finally as an elder will have changed as your life experiences are integrated into daily, weekly, and yearly rhythms of who and what you are and how you conduct yourself individually and with others.

If you have never thought about your personal vision, then the experience may be more daunting than if it is already a part of your life pattern. Don't let that stop you. Having a vision can make a tremendous difference in your life. Remember, vision can change you from feeling out of control to a person who has not only a sense of direction but a set of goals that are being acted on.

Getting started is most important. Realize that your personal vision is the picture or an image of your "true self." It should include who you want to be, how you want to feel and act, and whom you want to associate with. Your personal vision will let you see into the future, but it must always be grounded in the present.

The Johari Window Model is a very useful tool to help create your personal vision. It provides a framework for understanding who you are and how you "fit" into your personal world. Devised by Joseph Luft and Harry Ingham (1, 2) the model has been described as a "self-disclosure/feedback model of self-awareness."

The Johari Window Model

| | What others see or know | What others do not see or know |
|---|---|---|
| What I see or know | **1. The Public or Open Self** | **3. The Private (or Hidden) Self** |
| What I do not see or know | **2. The Blind Self** | **4. The Undiscovered Self** |

The Johari Window represents feelings, experiences, views, attitudes, skills, intentions, motivation, which are framed in terms of whether the information is known or unknown by you, and whether the information is known or unknown by others. In this model, "self" refers to you and "others" refers to individuals who are significant in your life (family, friends, work colleagues, etc.). The view is from four perspectives (or quadrants). They are:

1. **The public or open self is what is known by you and is also known by others.** This is the self that you choose to share with others. For example, your friends may know a lot about you, making your public/open self quadrant quite large. But, when you meet a new person, the size of this quadrant may be small until you have time to share more information about yourself. The aim is to always enlarge or widen this quadrant because it is here where you are the most effective and productive—free from mistrust, conflict, and misunderstandings.
2. **The blind self is what you do not know about yourself but is known by others.** These are things observed by others that you are not aware of. They can be positive or negative and can affect the way others act toward you. For example, you may have accidently gotten some food on your face when eating with a work colleague and are not aware of it, putting this information in your blind self quadrant. If the work colleague tells you about it (gives you feedback), the information moves from the blind self to the public/open self quadrant. If your work colleague is too embarrassed to tell you, the information will stay in your blind self quadrant. The consequence of staying there is that sometimes what others see and what you are blind to may cause untrue inferences, such as your colleague thinking, "what a sloppy eater." The aim is to always seek or solicit feedback from others to reduce the size of your blind self, making the open/public self quadrant larger. Discovery is accomplished through the use of authentic communication and active listening.
3. **The private or hidden self is what you know about yourself but others do not know.** These are the things you keep hidden from others for reasons that may include sensitivities, fears, or secrets. For example, you are able to play the piano but not well. You don't want your friends to know because they may ask you to play and you would rather not so you keep this talent hidden. If you tell your friends, this information moves from your private/hidden self to the open/public quadrant. Typically, people are more open with those they trust. The aim is to disclose and expose relevant information, thus moving it from the private/hidden to the public/open self quadrant. This promotes better understanding, cooperation, and trust and reduces the potential for confusion, misunderstanding, and poor communication. The extent of the disclosure of personal feelings and information is up to you. Some people are more willing and able than others to disclose. Remember, always disclose at a pace and depth that is "safe" for you.

4. **The undiscovered self contains things that nobody knows about you—including yourself.** This may be because you've never exposed this area of yourself, or because these things are buried deep in your subconscious. For example, you may have a natural ability or aptitude, but you are unaware of it, or you may have a fear but do not know its origin. A large undiscovered self quadrant would typically be expected in younger people, and people who lack experience. Trying new things, with no great pressure to succeed, is a way to discover unknown abilities and reduce the undiscovered self quadrant. As with disclosure and soliciting feedback, the process of self discovery is sensitive. The extent and depth to which you seek out discovery is up to you.

The significance and impact of the Johari Window Model on your life comes in the ever widening/enlarging of your open/public self quadrant, making the other three quadrants as small as possible. This is done by regular and honest exchange of feedback, and a willingness to disclose personal feelings. The examination of yourself through the use of the Johari Window Model allows you to understand what "makes you tick" and thus offers a platform for the creation and the maintenance of your personal vision.

Know that the process of personal visioning may be a risk for some. Why? Well, the reason is that what you may want to seek—your dreams and fondest desires—may be farther out of reach than what may appear to be realistic or do-able at the present. But, how will you know if you don't try? For some, risk taking is very easy. In fact, some people thrive on risk. Think about stunt people in the movies or other thrill-seekers. Risk is so pleasurable to them that it must always be incorporated into their daily lives.

For most, however, risk is at the least calculated if not a fear generator. In fact, some find they are risk aversive. These individuals experience physiological changes just thinking about risk and become desperately uncomfortable with feelings best described as unpleasant. Why does this happen? Risk taking challenges a variety of personal and professional "soft" zones that may include:

- Risk of failure
- Risk of embarrassment
- Risk of being hurt
- Risk of personal loss
- Risk of success

We can also become risk aversive because risk may not be promoted. Blessing-White asked employees if they were encouraged to take risks at work. Twenty-six percent of the employees asked said they were, but, sadly, 41% were not encouraged at all (3). It is no wonder that if risk is not reinforced in the workplace, many do not feel like doing it anywhere else.

*Only those who risk going too far can possibly find out how far they can go.*

*~T. S. Eliot*

Risk-taking fears and anxieties may also be based on perception and/or be cultural or learned barriers that may not be valid. Testing them is the key to moving forward. So living life is about taking risks, and risks are needed to identify and realize your personal vision. This is because risking is making the decision that you want something (4).

The first step in taking a risk is deciding you are willing to risk. You must look at all of the options and alternatives and know that you need to move forward. The next step is examining what you value. Values analysis is imperative because it allows you to find out what matters most to you. Values are the traits and qualities that are considered essential as they reflect your highest priorities and they are deeply held (5). Values are learned early and are influenced by those you associated with as a child, your friends, your experiences during school, what you read, as well as events both positive and negative during your work and adult personal life.

Values are your beliefs and often are determined by assessing specific attributes and qualities. To determine your values, it is helpful to look at a list of values and mark which are important to you. Ranking them is extremely helpful. Some examples of values include: teamwork, excitement, order, power, friendship, creativity, service, respect, honesty, and so on. Once you have identified what you value, you can then set your priorities.

Priorities can be difficult to set because many times the activities you need to be involved in compete with each other. Fulfilling these tasks may lead you to multi-tasking. Multi-tasking for many is very stressful and often not necessary because it occurs because priorities were not set. Priorities were not set because your personal vision is unclear. That is, your life path and journey is clouded and your direction is muddled. So creating a personal vision statement is essential. It illuminates your way and helps you make life and career decisions (6).

Know that once you have set your vision statement you are not done. You will need to determine priorities on a daily, weekly, monthly, and yearly basis. Some people find short-, mid-, and long-term goal setting a good way to go. For example, you may want to buy a house. Your short-term goal might be to identify where you would like to live, the mid-term would be to look at houses in that area to decide what type of house you would like, and the long-term goal would be to match your resources with the house you want and can afford to buy.

Remember to use your personal vision statement to guide your actions. For example, you find yourself in a meeting where you determine that your time is being wasted. Do you sit there and become frustrated, stressed, and angry? No, don't do that. Instead, think about your personal vision. Perhaps it is to engage more with people. So instead of thinking of the meeting as a time waster, "listen" to what people are saying and connect with them by engaging in the meeting. You might even change its direction to something that could be more productive!

You are now ready to create your personal vision statement. The remaining set of activities in this chapter will culminate in your statement. Be sure when you write your personal vision that it is written in the first person. You will notice that the place for your statement is limited, as it should be no longer than about 50 or so words, and anyone who reads it should be able to understand quickly and clearly where you are going and what you mean.

Enjoy the process, as here the risk is low and the payoff is high. When done, you will be excited to see where you want to go and what you want to do for the rest of your life!

## *Life Design Personal Visioning Checklist*

Reflect on the following to evaluate the extent to which you are currently ready to write your personal vision statement.

Close your eyes. See yourself in the future. It can be six months from now or years from today. Look at yourself. What you are doing, who you are with, what have you accomplished, what is important to you, and how are people interacting with you? Describe how you feel.

______________________________________________

______________________________________________

______________________________________________

What do most enjoy doing? Identify at least five things.

______________________________________________

______________________________________________

______________________________________________

List at least three identified strengths and weaknesses. Include the feedback you have received from others about these.

______________________________________________

______________________________________________

______________________________________________

Think about yesterday. What was the most important activity you were able to accomplish? Describe how you felt about that accomplishment.

______________________________________________

______________________________________________

______________________________________________

If you never had to work, how would you spend your time?

If you were at the end of your life, what would you regret not doing?

What risks have you taken in the last month? Were they new to you or were they something you have tried before?

What priorities have you set for yourself in the last month? Do they fit with your personal and professional desires?

## My Three Strategies

What I am willing to do today to realize my personal vision:

1. 
2. 
3. 

## Designer Activities

*(These activities will help you achieve your strategies.)*

*Personal and Professional Values*

- Think about what matters the most to you and list these.
- Identify five personal values.
- List five of your professional values.

*Risk Taking*

- Identify what you consider a risk.
- What makes it a risk to you?
- Does the level of risk stop you from trying to do what you desire? Why?
- What would help you take this risk?

*Setting Priorities*

- What are the top three priorities in your life?
- How do you decide on priorities?
- Is this approach successful, and, if not, what could make it successful?

*Getting Down to the Business of Writing*

Survey five individuals you most admire. Interview them and ask them to describe their personal vision and how it guides their lives. Use this information as research for your own personal vision statement and write it below.

| Personal Vision Statement |
| --- |
| |

# Personal Visioning
## REFLECTIVE JOURNAL

*Now that you have created your personal vision statement, use this Reflective Journal to write your "real" intentions for using your personal vision in your daily life. Don't forget to list any barriers you may encounter and how you will overcome them.*

## Reference

(1) Luft, J. (1969). *Of human interaction*. Palo Alto, CA: National Press.
(2) Luft, J., & Ingham, H. (1955). The Johari Window, a graphic model of interpersonal awareness. *Proceedings of the Western Training Laboratory in Group Development.* Los Angeles: UCLA.
(3) Laff, M. (2007, August). Risk taking culture is lacking in the US workplace. *Training and Development, 61*(8), 18.
(4) Baker, T. W. (2008). Risk taking for success. Retrieved from http://ezinearticles.com/?Risk – Taking -For-Success&id=1277132
(5) Heathfield, S. M. (n.d.). Success in life and work. Retrieved from http://humanresources.about. com/od/success/qt/values_s7.htm
(6) Heathfield, S. M. (n.d.). Create your personal vision statement. Retrieved from http:// humanresources.about.com/od/success/a/personal_vision.htm? p=1

## Other Readings to Explore

Capacchione, L. (2000). *Visioning: Ten steps to designing the life of your dreams*. New York: Tarcher.
Leider, R. J., & Shapiro, D. A. (1996). *Repacking your bags*. New York: Barnes & Noble Books.
Pedersen, R. P. (2000, September). Personal visions could offer a new paradigm. *Community College Week, 13*(2), 10.
Schwartz, J. (2008). *The vision board: The secret to an extraordinary life*. New York: Harper Collins.
Sullivan, D. (2006). *The laws of lifetime growth*. San Francisco: Berrett-Koehler Publishers.

# Your Future . . . Can Be Your Current Reality

You have now reached the end of the book, *Life by Personal Design: Limitless Horizons*, but by no means have you ended your journey!

You are to be admired and congratulated for the advances you have made in your journey so far. Your horizons will always be limitless. You just need to keep open to them. What we ask is that you continue to be mindful of yourself and your surroundings.

In closing, we have one more activity for you:

1. Revisit the Personal Design Quality of Life Wheel below and think about the percentages you would now place in each section. Compare these with the Wheel you did at the beginning of the book.
2. Review what you wrote in the Reflective Journals at the end of each chapter.
3. What specific intentions for change did you identify?
4. What barriers did you find, and did you overcome them?

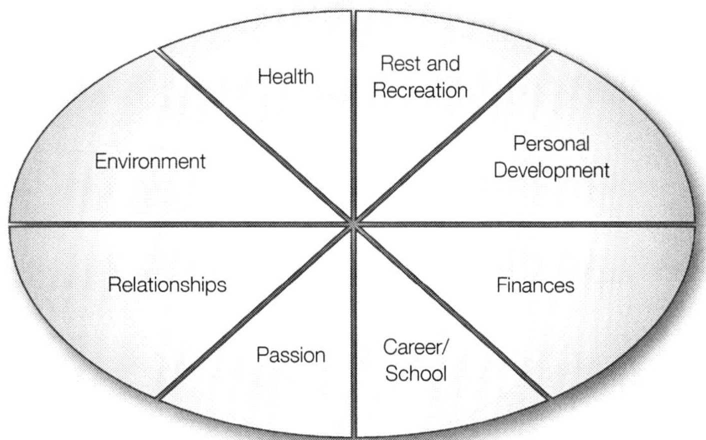


Personal Design Quality of Life Wheel

To continue to pursue a life of quality and fulfillment, we invite you to reflect on and then write your overall intentions for change for the next six months, for one year from now, and finally what you see yourself doing three years from now.

**Make your future a reality. Give yourself the gift of a Life by Personal Design!**